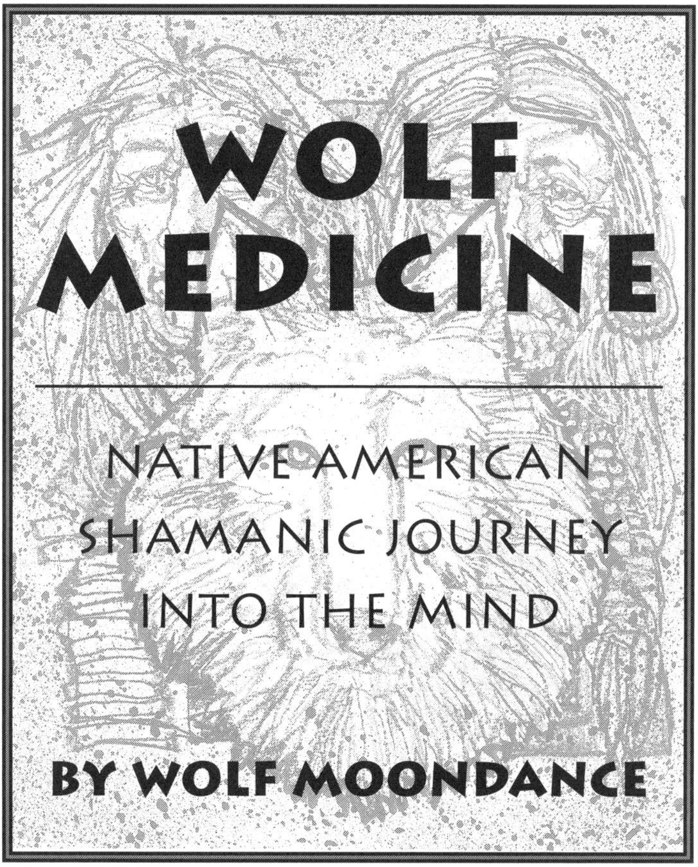

# WOLF MEDICINE

## NATIVE AMERICAN SHAMANIC JOURNEY INTO THE MIND

### BY WOLF MOONDANCE

Sterling Publishing Co., Inc.
New York

DEDICATED TO MYRTIE

8/19/1990 – 2/26/2000

*One who knows and one who learns. The Mind is the answer and when you step into the home of the stars, you go through the doorway of the mind to Star Song.*

**Library of Congress Cataloging-in-Publication Data**
Moondance, Wolf.
    Wolf medicine: Native American shamanic journey into the mind / Wolf Moondance; illustrated by Jim Sharpe and Sky Starhawk.
    p. cm.
    Includes index.
    ISBN 0-8069-3643-6
    1. Medicine wheels—Miscellanea. 2. Spiritual life—Miscellanea. I. Title.
BF1623.M43 W65 2001
        299'.7–dc21                                     2100-067063
                                                                                 CIP

Published by Sterling Publishing Company, Inc.
387 Park Avenue South, New York, N.Y. 10016
Text © 2001 by Wolf Moondance
Illustration © 2001 by Jim Sharpe and Sky Starhawk
Distributed in Canada by Sterling Publishing
<sup>c</sup>/o Canadian Manda Group, One Atlantic Avenue, Suite 105
Toronto, Ontario, Canada M6K 3E7
Distributed in Great Britain and Europe by Cassell PLC
Wellington House, 125 Strand, London WC2R 0BB, England
Distributed in Australia by Capricorn Link (Australia) Pty Ltd.
P.O. Box 6651, Baulkham Hills, Business Centre, NSW 2153, Australia

*Manufactured in the United States of America*
*All rights reserved*

Sterling ISBN 0-8069-3643-6

# CONTENTS

PURPOSE   7

PRELUDE   12

CHAPTER 1 ◆ THE NORTH GATE   15
*Cleansing Your Surroundings*   22
*Tools Needed in Doing Contemporary Shamanic Work*   22

CHAPTER 2 ◆ DARK EYES—BLUE CROW   24
*Tools for the Shamanic Journey*   32
*How to Know You Are On Your Sacred Path*   32
*The Calling of Your Sacred Path*   32
*Personal Neck Cloth*   35

CHAPTER 3 ◆ THE VOICE OF
GRANDMOTHER/GRANDFATHER WOLF   40
*The Rainbow Medicine Wheel*   49

CHAPTER 4 ◆ THE MAGICAL ONE—COLOR   52
*Color Teachings—Lizard Medicine*   62
*The Lesson of Trust—Scorpion Medicine*   63
*Ceremony of the Spirit Warrior*   64
*Color Medicine Bundle*   67
*Ceremony of the Medicine Bundle*   70

CHAPTER 5 ◆ DARK HEART—THE SNABBERS   72
*The Teachings of Energy—Badger Medicine*   83
*The Lesson of Limits*   84
*The Wolf's Eye Amulet*   85
*Vision of the Totem, Animal, Foot or Hoofprint*   87

### CHAPTER 6 ◆ THE BLUE-EYED RAVEN—PRAYER  90
*The Teachings of Prayer—Dolphin Medicine  98*
*Prayer Ties  98*
*Marriage Pot  99*
*Lesson of Expectations—Seal Medicine  102*

### CHAPTER 7 ◆ FLOWERS AND ICE—COURAGE  104
*The Teachings of Courage—Bee Medicine  112*
*Ceremony of Courage  114*
*The Lesson of Failure—Goose Medicine  115*
*Actions to Override Failure  117*

### CHAPTER 8 ◆ TEARS IN THE RIVER— UNDERSTANDING MEDICINE  119
*The Teachings of Understanding—Starfish Medicine  125*
*Ceremony of the Soul  127*
*The Lesson of Listening—the Bluebird  130*

### CHAPTER 9 ◆ WALKING THE RIVER—KNOWLEDGE MEDICINE  132
*The Teachings of Knowledge—Trout Medicine  139*
*Ceremony of the Inner Wolf  139*
*The Basket of Knowledge Stones  143*
*The Lesson of Forgiveness—the Mule  148*
*Note from Wolf Moondance  148*

### CHAPTER 10 ◆ THE WATERFALL OF JOY—HOME  151
*The Teachings of Will—Magpie  158*
*Soul Retrieval  159*
*Ceremony of Soul Recovery  163*
*Shamanic Soul Retrieval Journey  164*
*An Exercise in Soul Retrieval  165*
*The Lesson of Inner Peace—The Lightning Bug  168*

### CHAPTER 11 ◆ SWEET MEDICINE  170
*Prayer Bowl  177*
*Ceremony of Clearing the Mind  179*
*A Closing Note from Wolf Moondance  180*

WOLF TEACHINGS   181
*Colors   181*
*Colors of Wolf Medicine   181*
*Animal Spirit Teachings of the North   183*
*Lessons of the North   186*

ACKNOWLEDGMENTS   188

INDEX   189

# **PURPOSE**

When we look at the word "Mystery" and think about words like "secret," "misfortune," "sorrow," and "grief," when we embark on the endeavor of love and feel the unexplainable atrocity of hate, where are we? Caught somewhere between the mind and the brain.

"Oh, gee. I thought the mind and brain were all the same thing. Excuse me, how silly could I be to think that there is more than one component of thinking." Well, my purpose within *Wolf Medicine* is to explain that we have physicality known as the brain, and we have a spiritual experience known as the mind.

I want to take you to a place where you begin to understand, as in *Bone Medicine*, that physicality is spiritual. Presence and form and matter are all spiritual. We cannot separate them. I feel that we have divided everything there is to divide in our lives. We have divided practical from impractical, conditional from unconditional, religion from spirituality, education from Knowledge, and we have split everything down the middle. Well, we have two lobes in the brain, maybe one of them is the mind and one is the brain. We have a gland in our brain called the pineal gland. Maybe that gland is where the mind is and the rest is the brain.

I don't need any type of modern equipment to tell you what I know. From the first book I wrote to the books I will write after this, everything I tell you comes from my inner action with shamanic journey. When I go into the spirit worlds I listen and I go there with the intention to learn. What I carry is a gift that is older than Earth. I walk with the ancient Knowledge of spirit through shamanic belief. It cannot be proven or disproven. It cannot be destroyed. I walk with a Vision that I was given as a child. I have followed my mother's side of my life, and I have followed much of the Native American teaching in spirituality. Shamanism is not unique to Native Americans. It exists in every culture and every belief, for it is the voice of the mind—the spirit speaking through the brain. In *Wolf Medicine* it is the Wolf's job to show you the path of Truth. I think if you were to let go of your training and identify which part of the physical thinking apparatus you are using, you would say it is either the brain or the mind.

A great many experiments and a lot of research has taken place to bring forth a better understanding of the human brain, but very little has been done to understand the mind. When you say you feel something in your heart, or in your gut, you are speaking of what you hear in your mind. This reminds me of something my mother told me. I said to her one time, "Well, Mom, it's all in your head," and she said, "Well, where would you think it would be, in my butt?" She looked at me and smiled and added, "All thinking comes from the brain, which is the electrical charge mechanism that allows the mind to speak, which is the voice of spirit. Within your skull is a brain and from that brain everything happens. You don't think from your foot, girl."

As we experience life, understanding the North part of the medicine wheel is a necessity. And that's where we are, in the North section of the Rainbow Medicine Wheel—in the brain/mind/soul. It is easy to say my foot hurts, my stomach hurts, or I'm going to die because I have cancer or a disease, but what is really going on when we're sick is that something is malfunctioning in the brain. And it could have happened early in physical life—in your childhood—and gone undetected.

I cannot speak about the brain, because I am not a brain specialist. A brain specialist is a neurologist or psychiatrist. But I can speak about the mind because I am a mind specialist—a shaman. Shamanism understands the pathways of the neurological system, which are the movements within the brain. but the reason a shaman understands them is because shamans travel through the brain in the realm of spirituality. There are two specialists in the mind: the psychologist, who studies the mind and human behavior, and the shaman. The shaman lives in the realm where the voice of the mind originates, as well as in the world of physicality, for a shaman is a human being. But before a shaman was a human being, he or she was a spirit. It is imperative that a shaman knows that he or she existed as a spirit in the physical existence known as a lifekind.

A lifekind is the purest sense of spirit. It is pure energy that brings forth breath, which is our existence. A lifekind came before spirit and is pure Grandmother/Grandfather/Great Spirit/ Creator/God energy. Lifekind is where we come from and where we eventually go. Lifekind is the center of the spiral of life. All is lifekind. Where there is pure energy, that is a lifekind. Evil thoughts, wrongdoing, or hate is not a lifekind, but a mental reaction from anger or a disease. When humankind are practicing being angry or full of hate, a Choice has been made. The wrongdoing is a reaction to abuse. It isn't hard to be a lifekind. It is the pulsation that the spirit knows as breath.

The brain is the mechanism that causes all actions to take place in your physicality. If you're depressed, or if you're sick, or if you're scared, the brain is what you have to blame—not others, not philosophies, not spiritual paths, but the brain. The brain is made up of electrical charges and those electrical charges are energies—the pulsating, perpetual motions of life. So the brain is totally dependent upon life, and totally dependent upon perpetual motion. Perpetual motion and breath are Grandmother/Grandfather/Great Spirit/Creator/God.

The Wolf is a pathfinder. It is a leader. It is a teacher. That is what I am, spiritually and physically. In the physical form my body represents the Wolf for it is strong and it is large. My bones are thick and strong. My hearing is very finely tuned. My sight is keen and clear. My students speak of my words as being teeth that are sharp, that cut into your thinking pathways. Yes, I will Change your life. Yes, I have been called the last chance. Yes, I am one who lives in two worlds. I don't need anything but the Rainbow Medicine Wheel, for it is all there is. It has spirituality, it has education, it has fun, it has food—it is all. For life is a medicine wheel and when you step into the North section of the wheel you are dealing with the winter cold, you are dealing with eldership, with a time in your life when the end is soon, when things have weakened and died. Death and the end is the North part of the wheel.

It is important, as a wolf, that I lead you the right way. The teachings in this section are words that will make tremendous differences in your life. Everything that is physical comes to be because of the brain—the brain having the synapse process and the electrical transmitters that make it possible for electrical charges to take place in the right way. Everything works through the neurological system.

Understand that the brain runs on its own control mechanisms. Be careful when you start blaming doctors and others for killing people, and blaming others for making guns, and for dirty politics, because blame is a mental illness in itself. It's a mental illness because it is anger out of control. Where do emotions come from? They come from reactions within the mind that are created when the brain is not working properly in processing feelings.

And what are feelings? Reactions from the mind. What is the mind? It is several things. It is the doorway to the spirit where the feelings of the heart are. We do not feel and think in our heart—our heart is a muscle. It does not have any synapse processes or neurological reaction processes. It does not cause the neurological system in the body to work. It simply processes the blood. When we speak of heart, we are speaking of the mind. What we think of as "heart thought" is the mind. The mind is the doorway to the spirit, to the feelings, to the emotions. It is the place where all thinking emerges. Our heart is the life force of our body—the blood pump. We, as a lifekind, have a brain, and the brain is the home of the mind. One is physical—the brain, and one is spiritual—the mind. I know we speak of feeling things on a heart level, but my teachings come from the Medicine Wheel, and in Rainbow Medicine teachings, our brain is the mass that allows the mind to have thoughts.

I like to think of the mind as an opening—to infinity, to the eternal, to other worlds, to the other side. For this opening to take place, you must be mentally healthy. When you are not mentally healthy, you are not getting your thoughts fully processed. You do not have your memory solidly intact. You might not have the ability to have a conscience, or to have normal thinking patterns that reflect the realities around you.

When you allow yourself to accept the fullness of the North, you are facing the medicines of Color, Energy, Prayer, Courage, Understanding, Knowledge, and Will. The North section is the "mental" section. The word "mental" has been abused by narrowing it to refer to a person's being insane. Mental is brain/mind activity. We also suffer from the misuse of the term "mentally ill." As I see it, any time we are out of Balance, we are mentally ill. Any time we suffer from any sickness, we are mentally afflicted. Every human is mentally ill at some time in their lives in this day when we are all so often out of Balance. It is time, if we choose to heal humankind, that we accept the fact that everything is controlled by the mental plane, the brain. Remember, we don't think with our butt. The brain is an automatic stimuli that we must learn to respect.

The lessons of the mental section of the medicine wheel are those of trust, limits, expectations, failure, listening, forgiveness, and inner peace. As we look at each of these words, we will encounter spirit guides and inner totems that will help explain the conflict between the physical world, the brain itself, and spiritual thought, the mind. The medicine wheel is not just a structure that you look at on a one-dimensional basis. Your entire existence is a medicine wheel. I am very honored to have the contemporary Vision of the sun and the moon and the seven stars, for it allows me to step back into old traditions that have been forgotten. It allows me to reach forward and spread a star pathway for each of us to walk on. I do not claim to be traditional. I do not want to be traditional. For I am from today and tomorrow and much of what I teach is based on solid memories of yesterday.

When we deprive ourselves of our mind because we do not take care of our brain, we face sicknesses such as diabetes, heart failure, cancer, and we bring about emotions like spite, greed, and selfishness, and actions like thievery, abortion, and murder. All of these actions come from realms within our brain. Our brain gives us the ability to be healthy or unhealthy, and an unhealthy brain brings forth chemical imbalances that can cause us to crave sugar, alcohol, nicotine, and addictive drugs. We could even become addicted to spirituality, religion, education, or just simply watching movies or listening to music. For the behavior of addiction comes from a disease known as depression, which is serious, and many suffer from these chemical imbalances.

As I said before, I'm not an expert in the brain, but I am an expert in the mind. Our consciousness and our conscience, our memories—long term and short term—our reactions and our comparisons are what we are made of. It is interesting to think that a chair was a thought before it was a chair.

I hope that you understand that you are a mortal for a very short time, for the North speaks of death. First you are not here, then you are a child, then a young person, then an adult, then an elder. Then you cross the Rainbow Bridge for you have died, and you become an ascended elder, an ancestor. You are walking in the realm of the mind: you are in the memories of the ones you left behind and you live in the spirit world. You may be simply Energy, or Prayer, or Courage, or Understanding. Or you might return in the process of being the dirt, the wind, the fire, the ice, or pure energy. Life, as I said, is the perpetual motion of existence and physicality is a part of that.

We each have a soul. Through our loss of Balance and short-term memory problems, through fear and pain, we lose touch with our soul. The human soul is a spiritual connection with Great Spirit/Creator/God. When we are mentally in Balance, we are rich and full, healthy and happy. Our soul is the path we follow. A strong soul is a strong medicine path.

I hope you enjoy the teachings and the ceremonies that lie ahead of you in the North section of the Rainbow Medicine Wheel.

Aho.

# PRELUDE

In shamanism we work with four realms—three of them are popular in contemporary shamanism: the Upper World, the Middle Reality, and the Lower World. The fourth realm is the other world—the world of red, orange, yellow, green, blue, purple, and burgundy.

In a lot of shamanic teachings, the other world is viewed only as the Mystery. I like to view it as the spirit world within the Mystery. The other world is the seventh position around the center stone within the Rainbow Medicine Wheel. When you embark upon the path of shamanism, it is important to remember that everything happens in your brain. Your brain gives you the ability to comprehend, to discern, to manifest, to have ability, to bring forth, to know, to think, to reason, and to fantasize. Emotions—especially the primary ones—anger, disgust, happiness, sadness, acceptance, fear, and joy—are the answer to the question, "Where does evil come from"? They are also the answer to flow, goodness, kindness, and everything else you have in your human existence. Such thoughts as evil and hate are complex emotions.

Everything that we are physically depends upon our brain. Without our brain, we have no life. Often we think of our heart as being our life support. But our life support is a tie between the heart and the mind. The mind is the Mystery, the home of the spirit and soul. In the study of modern science, the facts of the spirit are not understood. The human soul is a mystery to science. In Shamanism, it is easy to understand that the soul is the spiritual pathway to life.

It has been only lately that we have come to understand that we have an aura, and that people have begun to believe that positive Energy, Prayer, respect and honor are the key points of existence. I know that when the brain is damaged and cannot function, life is over, because there is no other system of transmission that can enable the rest of the body to react. The human body is a reaction to the brain, and the brain is a home to the mind, and the mind is the transmitter of the soul and the will to goodness as well as evil.

I like to think of evil as being simply Choices and actions. I think of the darkness as a deeper shade of blue and purple. I believe that the lower world, where our fantasies and our connections to imagination are, is the place where the powers of ugly, bad, wrong, death, hate, dishonor, disrespect, and evil come from. I believe that the most evil thing there is, is ignorance. When we don't know answers or care to understand others, the way we live is in ignorance. In ignorance, we live evil lives.

The visions in this particular work are connected to mental issues—the issues of death, evil, wrong, disrespect, disobedience, unforgiveness, and conditionality. These issues are reactions that have come from harbored grudges, blaming, and fear-motivated actions. They are the sicknesses known as mental illness. We will be dealing with rejection and denial. I believe it is very important spiritually, as well as physically, that we start to understand mental health, and that the only horned being that exists is an animal in the woods. I think it is important for us to stop using the word "witch," and stop drawing lines between witchcraft and Christianity and shamanism. I think it is important for people to understand that if we are going to enjoy the fullness of the blue world, which is where we live, we must come to harmony, and that harmony is peace, inner peace—a lesson that is hard to learn.

As you embrace Wolf Medicine, you will embrace your own fears. You will be challenged to accept your mental disabilities. You will be uplifted, enlightened, and enriched in the vibrations of the Colors, the experiences of Prayer, and the depth of Understanding and Knowledge that lies ahead of you. Fear not mental illness, for it is treatable. Reach out to spirituality for serenity and comfort. Reach out to neurology and psychiatry for support and Understanding. I condone nothing but the sacred circle of Truth—be it scientific or spiritual. For us to endure the horrendous diseases, to face the most god-awful fears, we must draw upon our mind, and its teachings will be the ones that live beyond in the other world.

Aho.

# 1 ◆ THE NORTH GATE

It is midnight. Quiet has come to the Lodge. The students have come once more, to decide if they will walk to a new section in the Rainbow Medicine Wheel. I have listened to their intentions and heard their desires. They are seven strong, good people. It isn't easy, Grandmother/Grandfather, to watch the struggles of the students. Can you show me, so that I will understand, how to guide each these students on the path of the Rainbow Medicine Wheel?

I lie down on the ground. I feel its coldness, for Winter has come. I take a deep breath in and out. Looking to the North gate, I see the wind is blowing the white flag. The wind is from the North. I hear the rattling of bells and smell the sweet grass and sage.

Before me is a familiar path. It is covered with snow, icy and dark. I begin to follow it. I give thanks for my warm skin shoes and the buffalo robe that is wrapped around me. And I follow the path.

I walk upwards, way up, into the spirit world. I stand in the howling wind. The snow pierces my face. I feel a coldness deep inside, the stillness of black, the bleakness of white, for they are the same in the North — black and white. I hear the wind swirling around me, and laughter from the snowflakes. A soft voice bids me welcome. I hear it in the snow. "Welcome."

I'm cold. My hands feel as if they are solid ice and I take a shallow breath. I cannot breathe deeply, for it is too cold. I don't think I can travel any further.

"Oh yes," a soft voice says. "You must. It is the North gate, and not far is the one you seek. The story of your life is understood in the North."

I feel very sleepy. As I go to take a step, my foot is heavy. So are my hands. I'll lie down here in the snow, and find comfort in my thick, warm buffalo robe. I sink to the ground and cover myself. My buffalo robe makes a small tent-like structure for me to stay cuddled inside. I feel the force of cold trying to penetrate my skin. I go deep, very deep, into dark purple and dark burgundy. I can hear my heart beat. Then the sound fades away and there is nothing but stillness. I take very shallow breaths. The swirling wind speaks words of comfort.

"Do not worry, Wolf. The North will teach you. Listen and hear."

I hear a very large sound and feel a very large presence. I cannot open the buffalo robe for I'll freeze.

"That is the problem," a deep voice rings out. "It is the problem with all human two-leggeds—they do not to wish to take a chance. Fear is an intelligent movement, for if you open the robe you die. Open the robe. You're dead anyhow."

I lie there very still. "I wonder why I'm referred to as dead?"

"You must step through death to listen. You cannot learn the lesson of listening without death. There are many forms of death—transmutation, transformation, transparency, invisibility, and as death, a doorway."

"But I don't want to die," I reply.

The Bigness speaks in Solid words. I feel as if they burn when they touch me.

"What will happen to you is you will fear in the physical realm, and what will happen to you in the spirit space—where you are—is you will let go of your robe. You must remember that you are in spirit, for you have walked the path. When you come to spirit or spirituality, you have no control, for there is no need for control. You have gone beyond your physicality, and through your mind you have traveled to a place in spirit where you confront your soul. Wolf Moondance, you know your students come to you for answers. They wish to know. In their human life they must use intelligence and have common sense to hear spirit and know how to use Color in their life."

"Who are you?" I ask.

"It is simple who I am. I am the voice. You see, there are many components in the spirit realm. The voice is the teacher. It is what you are—a wolf. It is what they seek, the one who knows, the voice, the path. Some refer to it as education. Some refer to it as intelligence. Some refer to it as knowing. Some refer to it as the great Understanding, the spiritual path. It is the North gate. The voice opens the way, and that is me."

The voice is silent. All I can hear is the breath of the wind.

"Is that you? Is the breath, the wind, you?"

"Yes," the voice answers.

A crystal, cold, clearness is what I hear—deep, solid, and intense—a constant roar. Everything could be penetrated by the clarity of this voice.

"I feel as if you could blow everything off the Earth."

"I can!" the voice says, deep and strong.

"I do not wish to come out from underneath this robe because I feel as if you will blow me away."

"You cannot avoid the learning that lies before you. You must understand death. You must stand in the Fullness of the self, a hollow bone. You have walked the road past Bone Medicine. You have seen the body and know that it is weak. You also know that it can be separated from the bone. It is time to stand in the whiteness and be nothing but the bone."

There is a gust, a powerful gust of wind, that blows the robe open, and I am standing unprotected in the cold—the deepest, burning cold I have ever felt. Now the colors start, first the gold comes, bright and powerful. It coats my body and I feel myself separate. I am no longer flesh and blood and muscle. I stand as bone. Now comes blue light—a powerful light that coats the bone, and my skeleton glows. I watch the light as it bathes my

bones. Now an intense silver energy emerges. I walk forth from the bone and I am pure light. I can feel the cold giving me Strength and holding me intact.

I look down at the silver shimmer of myself. I see it in my hand. Even though there is no muscle or bone, the light forms an arm and a hand, and it is connected to a pulsating vibrant, sparkling body.

"Voice," I call out.

"Yes."

"This is incredible!" I look at where my feet are and they are still my feet, but they are glistening and sparkling. "This is wonderful!"

"Yes," the voice says. "Once you have walked past death, you stand in all the radiant Beauty of Color and Energy that is."

"I love this spirit world. I love coming here. I love the Beauty and the ability to be free. I love the fact that I can float and fly. I love it that I can walk on water. I love the way the animals talk and the rocks teach."

"Yes," the voice replies. "But in transmutation something is lost when something is gained. It is important that you remember that you have reached the North section of the medicine wheel. In it is the answer to night and day, the answer to life and death."

As the voice speaks, I hear the constant roar of the wind at hurricane force. A blizzard surrounds my existence. I watch the tree people bend with the force of the wind. Each one of them is coated with crystals of ice and snowflakes that pile onto the limbs like whipped cream.

"It is remarkable, Voice, that in the spirit world it is the same as in the physical world."

"It only looks the same, because that is how your brain comprehends the mind. Nothing is the same. Look and see."

I heard the swirling sound of the wind and millions of beings laughing. The sound spirals and moves in a circle around my head.

"Voice," I call out.

But there is no answer, only the roar of the wind. I look back and there is my robe in its little tent shape, but I am no longer cold.

Before me on the ground I see a long crystal rod. To the side of it is a long turquoise rod. These rods lie in the snow. They are beautiful. I want to pick them up, but I know that when you are in the spirit realm you must be very careful what you take and what you hold.

"Grandmother/Grandfather Spirit, can you hear me? Grandmother/Grandfather Wolf, are you here?"

There are no words—nothing but the two rods in the silver moonlight.

I bend down and pick them up—the crystal one in my left hand and the turquoise one in my right hand. They glisten and become warm. The one in my right hand speaks.

"Hello."

"Hello," I say.

"Thank you for picking me and my sister up."

"You're welcome."

"Why did you pick us up?"

I think for a moment. "It is appropriate in the spirit world to pick things up. It is appropriate to work with them. It is appropriate to hold them. And I know that I might have to lay you down soon and go home to my physical existence while you stay here in the spiritual one."

"It is not that way for you," the turquoise rod says. "You will keep us. You will put us in your spiritual medicine bag and carry us with you, for in the mind you must have Balance, and we are the rods of Balance. I am the stone of physicality and my sister is the stone of spirituality. She is crystal and I am turquoise. You may call me Turq."

"I am very glad to meet both of you," I say. "Is there a reason why you have appeared to me?"

"Yes," Turq says. "You must have protection in your mind. You must have the Understanding that the brain has limits and that is where death is."

"Well, Turq, I've been approached by death. It has visited me in the physical realm and it has scared me gravely. My whole life I have dealt with death. It has taken many of my loved ones. Is there anyone in the physical realm who doesn't deal with it?"

"No, there isn't, and that's why you will need me. I am protection. I am the voice of Great Spirit. Listen and Balance will come."

"You're the voice," I say, looking at the rod.

"I am one who is the Voice, that is true. Turquoise and Fire are the voice of Great Spirit. They are the protecting forces that allow you to remember. As you walk your human existence, you'll come to times when there is a need for transformation. You cannot hold on and comfort yourself with another being. You cannot use marriage, children, and Success to stabilize your existence. You must understand that your existence is eternal and needs no stabilizing. It is my job to help you understand this as we walk through the realm of the North."

I feel a warm tingle in my left hand. I look at Crystal. "Hello," I say.

A soft, tinkling voice speaks back. "Hello. I am so glad that you have reached the point where we can speak. I know that as you've walked through the mind, you've stepped into the realm of spirit. The answers of your soul will sing to you. Wolf, it may be hard to understand at times, for you will hear other stories, but an elder is Wisdom. The eldership of a human being comes in old age, and it is the most wonderful time, for the wind blows through your life."

As Crystal speaks, snow spills from one of the tree limbs. The other trees gently drop their snow. The coldness of Crystal is deep and penetrating in my left hand, but I feel a warmth in my bones.

"That's right," she says. "You will be warm always because of our connection. You will be cold always because of our connection. When you feel the coldness, it is a time for you to pay attention. Emptiness and coldness are real. Death is not always a doorway—it can be a transformation into the lower world from which you can never return. Look."

Before me I see a cave. It is blue inside the opening. The blueness becomes deep and dark as I look into it.

"Walk in the cave," Crystal says, and I begin to walk. As I step through the cave entrance, I feel the darkness and the cold—deep, brutal cold.

"Don't be afraid", Turq says. "'Don't be afraid' simply means accepting. You are going within the darkness of what people call the mind, but it is the brain. The brain is dark and still."

As I step into the cave it glistens. Sparks of lightning shoot all around me. It is intense. The flashes of light are yellows and greens, oranges, blues, and purples. I cannot breathe. My throat feels tight and constricted. I think of the snow and relax. Crystal becomes very warm in my left hand, and Turq becomes very cold in my right.

"It is possible for us to switch positions," Turq says. "It is important that you relax your intensity, for the North is no lightweight place. The brain is all that a human being is, but we are in the mind. We have stepped beyond."

**I hear the howl of the wolf calling me back.**

# CLEANSING YOUR SURROUNDINGS

When you are going to do spiritual work, it is important to cleanse your aura, to clear your mind, to focus your thinking, and to bring about a centered, grounded way of thinking. This is done by smudging. It is called the Ceremony of Sacred Herbs. To smudge, you take a small amount of cleansing herbs—sage and sweet grass—light them and let them smolder in a fireproof bowl or a shell. Let the smoke rise. With your hand or a fan move the smoke around your body. It is important to breathe the smoke in. The herbs will open and strengthen your third eye chakra.

Your third eye chakra is located in the center of your forehead. The smudging with herbs will allow a centering to take place in your physicality, balancing your positive and negative ions. As the smoke passes around you, be sure to move it beneath your feet and behind your back and totally around your body. At the same time, allow the smoke to work in its electric way, moving Energy within the spirit. Take occasional deep breaths, and relax.

When the smudging is done, you will feel very centered and solid. Continue breathing softly and know that you are ready to enter Ceremony in a good way.

# TOOLS NEEDED IN DOING CONTEMPORARY SHAMANIC WORK

When you are studying shamanism or working with *Wolf Medicine*, it is important to understand the word "medicine." In a physical way it is something that you take to bring about a Healing. It is usually thought of as being pills, liquids, or herbs, but in *Wolf Medicine*, it is thoughts, deeds, actions, and words. There are several tools often used in shamanic work.

You will need candles in all seven colors (red, orange, yellow, green, blue, purple, and burgundy) plus white. You will need a journal, which is any form of paper or a place on a computer where you keep your writings, or a tape recorder where you keep your thoughts. You will need a medicine blanket or shawl that you wrap yourself in to keep warm. It is important to keep your back covered in the physical realm when you are opening up in front in the spiritual realm. When you open yourself in the front, you will be working with your heart and solar plexus chakras. These are energy points located at your heart and in the center of your stomach area.

Other things needed are quiet places in your home or a safe place in some building where you will not be disturbed, or a quiet place outside in your yard or a park, or camping area, where you will not be disturbed mentally or physically.

You will need your sacred herbs, such as sweet grass or sage, to burn in your smudging Ceremony, as well as a fireproof bowl or abalone shell.

It is a good idea to wrap different types of stones in 100% cotton cloth. Stones that you might use in your thinking processes during Ceremony would be crystal, turquoise, picture jasper, obsidian, fluorite, hematite and any other stones that you find valuable in your own personal work or that you might have worked with previously and know the meanings of.

Your spiritual tools are transitional objects. They are used to help you do shamanic work until you have the Confidence to do it without them. They are going to enable you to tell brain reality from mind reality.

Each object you use working with shamanism is a point of connection. It enables you center your thoughts and allow yourself to Balance your physicality so that you can detach from it. You need a detaching motion in order to switch from brain reality to mind reality. I know that ordinary world teachings tell us that the mind and the brain are the same thing, but in *Wolf Medicine* I would like us to reach out in Knowledge and vastness and experience the true brain reality and mind reality.

Shamanism is based on two worlds—one physical reality and one spiritual. reality. The brain—the physical reality—is electric, magnetic and complicated. You'd have to go deeply into science and study chemistry as well as physics and neurology to be able to understand the Power of the human brain. Humans are very limited in their memories and their Knowledge of the brain and physical reality, so psychiatry and psychology are very young fields, while mind reality—shamanism—is very old. Shamanism is pure, because you are not working with physical reality. You are working with the attributes of perpetual motion, eternal realities, spiritual dimensions, celestial and elemental relationships, as well as spirits who cannot be seen or defined.

In shamanic practices, working with the upper, lower, and middle realities, your experiences will be very vivid. In the other world, nothing is ever forgotten, whereas in physical reality, the brain's filing system is often faulty. For example, what is known as a dream is almost always hard to remember.

Aho.

# 2 ◆ DARK EYES— BLUE CROW

Peacefulness surrounds us. It is Winter, the time of the white flag—the North gate. The seven students sit in a circle, knowing that they have entered the realm of the mind.

I feel a restlessness in the room. I see the students wondering as each one of them eagerly waits.

"You might be seeking Native American beliefs or truths. That might be why you have come, but by now, walking the medicine wheel in the way that you have and standing at the North gate, I need to tell you the story of the crow. I need to show you the heart of the one who speaks. Because Native American culture is a way of magic. It is the doorway to natural Healing through shamanism. It is the walk of the crow.

"As we walk with the fear of death in the quest of life, searching for the Truth of life, we live the story of the crow. As we fear that shamanism is living in two worlds, we learn the story of the crow. The crow is dark and the story is the Strength of the crow."

I remember the story the way my mom told it to me:

> When the night is dark, you are standing in the mind of the crow.
>
> When the fear of life is around you, the crow watches. We as a people are weak and we all want proof that Great Spirit is Real. Well, long ago there was a Young One who went off to find Great Spirit.
>
> But instead of going to the upper world where Great Spirit was waiting to greet him, the Young One went to the underworld. It was the wrong Choice, because no one was supposed to go to the underworld. The Dark One waited there to steal their souls.
>
> As he entered the lower world, the Young One was in great danger. The darkness came across him, and he had never known such fear. He felt frozen as the fear grew tight around him. He heard the sound of thunder and a strong wind coming for him. In front of him was a gray mist and strange lights.
>
> As he stood there in fear of the Dark One, he felt himself changing.
>
> The Dark One came close and the Young One heard his voice.
>
> " Why was I called here? It is only a crow. The crow is nothing but the keeper of the records of life. I see the answer is death and that makes me happy," the Dark One said.
>
> "Good to see you, crow, are you coming to the lower world for lessons now? I know that you are the warning of death and I welcome the soul you are bringing me."
>
> The Dark One was very close. The Young One was standing in front of him. He could see his reflection in the Dark One's eye. He saw a crow—but the crow was blue!
>
> The fear fled from the Young One's heart. He knew that blue was Understanding, and that the way of the Crow was Truth.

The Dark one left and the Young One went on with his life, knowing that he had the color of blue and the Truth of Great Spirit. He knew that the Crow is strong in Truth and Understanding and that it could walk in two worlds. The Young One had seen Great Spirit in his own Strength.

I remember the one with the familiar dark eyes. The one who called me to remember my heritage. He stands there in his complexity. His strong shoulders carry the weight of the world, and in his deep, dark eyes I seek the answers.

I breathe in and out, and relax. I feel the freedom of letting go of the physical reality. I stand on a path of stars. There is a red one. I step. An orange one, I step there. And I continue walking on yellow, green, blue, purple, and burgundy. The stars become a glistening path, twinkling and sparkling—colors of turquoise and coral, colors of peach and mauve—shimmering diamonds on my pathway. The snow is deep. The time is cold. There is no need for moments or hours, for I am in spirit, and all around me the darkness is a deep shade of purple. It becomes deeper in burgundy, and I walk. I feel the snow deep on my calf. It is hard to walk.

I stand at the river and the shoreline is ice. The water sparkles as it rushes through the ice. I want to hear his voice, the deep sound of Truth.

"Come to me. Come to me, Dark Eyes," I say. "I long to hear your deep voice."

The familiar laugh rings out, deep and suggestive, and I feel his warm hands on my shoulders.

"Ah, you have returned. I knew you would." He spins me around and I look into those dark eyes. He has changed—old now. His face is wrinkled, road maps of the stories he holds in his heart. He is still strong and his chest is thick. His hair is white, pulled back in a long braid. The end of the braid is wrapped in white cloth, with small strings of rag. His face is thinner, his hands are wrinkled with age. He has on a coat made of coyote skin and on the lapel hang four black feathers. He wears blue jeans with a belt that has a beautiful buckle made of turquoise. His boots reach up to his knees and are made from leather, laced, and tied all the way up. They have wolf hair around the tops.

"You have come again, home to the river," he says. "I waited for you, to tell you one more thing." He places his hand on my cheek, and I look deep into his eyes. "You are the white wind," he says. "You cross the ground with elegance. You walk with a legacy of the sun and the moon and the stars. There are those who so seek the right way that their hearts are empty and your howl calls them. I will send you to a place and a time where you will see yourself. Walk to the white flag and step through the gate. There you will be within your thoughts. There you will find the diamond road—some call it the silver cord. It is a road of diamonds with sparks of color."

He holds out his hand and in it are seven diamonds. They turn to seven colored stars. He throws them in the air and before me I see the familiar path, a rainbow that glistens, inviting me to walk on it. I follow it. Walking in the snow, I feel his presence.

"I have missed you. I always miss you," I say to him.

He laughs. "There is no sense in missing me for I am always in your heart. We are the same, we two, yet different—the North and South. You, the White Wind, the North, and me, the Yellow Sky, the sun, the South. You have come to a time where I am no more, past this day."

"What do you mean?" I ask.

There is snow in his beard, which has turned white with age.

"Death would be easy. There is no death for me. What you see is closure. Here in the North, it's time for you to accept."

I feel a distance between us.

"You are facing Understanding," he says.

"That's not easy, for I have never understood us."

"It's time," he says, "for you to concentrate on where you're at and what you have learned. This is what we are—knowing." He looks ahead. "This is the home of the wolf."

I look ahead and there is the most magnificent sight I have ever seen. The mountains are rugged and tall, covered with snow, hidden behind clouds. At their base, streams of water sparkle with yellow hues. The ground is covered with deep snow. Clouds shift and the mountain tops peek through them like ghosts through a window. I am engulfed in this magical moment. I am home. The white flag is blowing on the gate.

"You must step beyond now, and walk without me."

A raven circles above us. Dark Eyes looks up and says, "That is the one you seek. You see, the medicine wheel on earth is only a symbol. It is a place where you can understand the center, where you come before the sacred directions. It is a place where the lessons lay their stories at your feet. You either learn them, or you suffer. It is a place where the medicines speak to your heart. You walk them each day—the truths, the medicines," he says.

I see a sadness in him, growing stronger.

"You think that it's over. But the Truth is that you are about the teach-

ings of my heart. You must not fear, because there is nothing that can separate us. But you have a life and that will be a hard lesson for you. What is going to happen is the completion of a circle. Can you see that? Understand, wherever you go, that the North and South is one line, for the heart is the mind."

"Why is it that I feel that we'll be separated?"

He looks at me and smiles. "That's the problem. Human beings separate everything. You and I can never be separated, but you must see the completion of the wheel."

"How bad will it hurt?" I ask.

"As much as you want it to."

He looks frail to me, and faint.

"Why? Why are you fading?" I ask.

"Seek out the Blue-Eyed Raven, for you know him as your Balance. The Wolf and the Coyote do not walk as a match. We are not an 'us,' we are not even a 'we.' You are you and I am me," he says.

"So what you are saying is that we are not soul mates, I guess." I look into the depth of his eyes—deep, dark, black marbles.

"No, what you and I hold is similar to brother and sister. I guess you could say we are cousins, for the Wolf and the Coyote are the same in that they have four legs and two ears, sharp teeth, and a thick coat. But we are very different, male and female. We are very different, the Wolf and the Coyote. You are the brain, the mind, the soul. I am the Coyote, the emotions, the innocence, the playfulness. Do you know who we are now?"

I feel the wind spiraling around me. Huge snowflakes fall like feathers. Everything is shimmering. I see shooting stars in the day sky.

It is time that you finish the path, for here we stand in the center and there you go in the North gate. There are those who walk the medicine wheel and listen to your words. It is I who set confusion at their feet. I give them Choices of passion and romance, drugs and alcohol. You give them Choices of breath and eternity. I give them the Choice of walking on in the West and dying. You give them the Choice of the North and eternal life. I leave you now. No more dances at the river. The time for me to leave is a time for you to wake up and know life is thoughts. I have no more thoughts of you."

"No," I say.

"We are different as night and day," he says. "You are the night and I am the day. The love affair that you think you have is nothing more than the rest of the road. Nothing here is permanent—not marriage, not soul mates, not even friendship. Beyond the North gate is your totality. You walk to the center. Listen, for Sweet Medicine sings to you."

"Sweet Medicine?" I look at him and say. "Sweet Medicine. What are you talking about?"

"You'll see," he says.

His eyes have become stars, green ones. Sparks of light fly from them. He changes to King Coyote and then back to Dark Eyes.

"You walk with the Blue-Eyed Raven, for he is Magic. Go. Go now, and understand that everyone is looking for answers. But what they think they are in love with might simply be their emotions. You've always thought that we were meant to be, but what we are is eternal twins."

I take a deep breath and lightning sparks as it hits the ground before me. Thunder roars across the mountains. There is a tremendous snow storm high in the magnificent ones. I don't want to walk beyond the North gate. I don't want to leave him.

"I am a human," I say. "I don't understand any of this."

He laughs his deep laugh, the one I remember from when we danced on the river. "You see, Wolf, we have been together forever. The sky and the earth—me the earth and you the sky. There is nothing that dances like us, for the Red Road is not the Blue Road. We are the physical story. The Red Road is the spiritual way—your life that you live as a teacher. You have come to your eldership. You stand in the North, where it is now midnight. Death has come and you have no physical existence."

I look at him and say, "Am I dead? Is this medicine wheel thing death?"

"Heh," he laughs. "You are so, so hard to teach, Wolf. We stand, one of two, and there are the others." He points his hand and I see an eagle circling above us. "There. The eagle represents enlightenment—the time when you came to your Grandmother/Grandfather Wolf and walked on the river. It is time now," and he points to the west. "There is the one."

I see the bear, the Grand grizzly, the keeper of the wheel, the chief, the wise elder of Life, the one who walks as physicality.

"There is the Red Road, the pathway, the path of spirit and enlightenment and introspection. There are the emotions, the brain, mind, and soul, and all of us are the medicine wheel. We stand in Balance."

He extends his hand and I hold onto it. I hear the wind, the tinkling of bells, the clatter of the rattle, the crackling of the fire. I see the circle of students gazing into it, voices of the ancient ones speaking stories into their minds. One wants to know about marriage, and one wants to know why they are going their own way after so long, and one wants to know why her half-side had to die so soon; it seems like yesterday they started their walk together. And one simply takes a deep breath and embraces the Truth.

"Those students, they listen, and we are their voice. I speak to them of happiness and fear, of disgust and joy. You show them, White Wind, you show them, Wolf, the pathway through the magical realms of the Rainbow Medicine Wheel. Each one of them cries out for Knowledge."

As he holds my hand I feel it grow colder.

"You must follow the Crow, the deepest of blue, for it is the way of the shaman."

I feel myself aging. I turn and look at that beautiful view, the home of the ancient ones, the home of the wolf.

"You are free now. Follow the Blue-Eyed Raven to the center of Sweet Medicine. I will always......" his voice drifts away.

I follow the path deep into the moonlight, into the night. I think in just a moment the day will come and he will be here again.

"No. I will always...." I hear whispers in the wind.

A different voice speaks very clearly. "Through the North gate you have come. You have stepped through death and you are now in the upper world. Listen."

I hear the caw of a crow and I look into a tree. An enormous crow is sitting in it, silhouetted against the midnight sky. I see the blackness in the silver full moon. I have walked through the North gate. A black and white horse charges past me, crossing the Rainbow Bridge. I stand in the spirit world.

**I hear the howl of the wolf calling me back.**

# TOOLS FOR THE SHAMANIC JOURNEY

The journal is a spirit journal. It is any notebook in which you can keep your reflections and memories. In the old day it was a pictograph, pictures were painted on a skin—symbols that represented the dreams and Visions of the people. These Visions and dreams guided them, as yours do today. When you keep a journal it is important to write down the ideas that guide you. Life is often hard to understand for it is a lesson, a lesson of the West. It is our physicality and that is only a small part of our existence. It is important to take notes in your spirit journal about your shamanic journeys and about your lessons in life. As humans, we take life for granted; and our spirit journal helps us to understand that life is not a lightweight lesson. Understanding the value of life is one of the things you will achieve by keeping a spirit journal.

# HOW TO KNOW YOU ARE ON YOUR SACRED PATH

What is a sacred path? Is it your religion? Your personal philosophy? Is it the teachings you receive from your elders and your family members? I can tell you what it isn't. It isn't jealousy. It isn't greed. It isn't envy. And it isn't the walk of material existence. When you enter the final stages of life, you cannot show your legacy by how much you own, for there is nothing worthy about ownership.

The sacred path is made up of magical teachings. It is the medicine stones that we know as the Rainbow Medicine Wheel. It is the teachings that an old one passes on to a young one. It is living life in its purest form, breathing fresh air and walking in Confidence—knowing that the Balance of life is sacred, and that Creativity brings forth life. You will know that you are on the sacred path of life when you feel a deep joy and happiness each day as you draw breath.

The sacred path is a place in which you take space and make Prayer. It isn't about how hard you work. It is about what the work is—the teaching, the Healing, the presenting, the Creativity of life. It's about stepping into the lessons of each day, for there never is a day on the sacred path that there is not a lesson. You can hear the voices of purpose and unity, originality and faith, Sincerity and reason, worth, clarity, poise, and discipline. These are lessons—the grandest things that are passed on as an experience. Account, fact, sense, and complete, purpose, obedience, life, and action. Solid, full, and worthy. Lessons walk you into the realms, places where you find sense through trust and limits; freedom from expectations and failure; listening, forgiveness, and inner peace. You have walked the Rainbow Medicine Wheel of lessons. You have stepped on the sacred crosswalk, the sacred path, your reason for being.

Why do you do what you do? That is what the pathway is about. Is it the path of sorrow, ignorance, and mental illness? Or is it the path of sacredness, dignity, and honor? Do you bow your head in sadness and regret? Or do you stand in the totality of your Strength? The sacred pathway is the honor of life. It is Accountability, Responsibility, Sincerity, Honesty, Respect, Commitment, and the Mystery of life.

As the eagle soars and the hawks circle watchfully in the sky, the old bear lies lazily in the sun. The coyote slips along the edges and the wolf walks with pride and impeccability. These are the steps of the path that we know as our sacred existence.

## THE CALLING OF YOUR SACRED PATH

We all like to say we are on the path. A lot of us say we are on the Good Red Road. The Good Red Road is a way of living in which you use no drugs, no alcohol, you bring no harm to another, you wish no evil on anyone. You never try to get even; you are never sad or upset about what someone else has or does. You walk with integrity and honor. The Good Red Road is a place where you live your life in accordance with your spiritual beliefs. You follow the laws and principles of spirit. You love others as you do yourself. You walk with the truths and teachings of the Holy One.

When you have a sacred path, you have purpose. You have learned the lesson. Purpose is a lesson. You have clarity. You have learned the lesson of clarity. You have patience. You have learned the lesson of patience. You have trust. You have learned to trust. It is important to know that when you have your calling and your sacred path, your life is known and your acceptance of life reveals your values and qualities. Everything you do, you do in a good way.

If you are looking for your path, get out your journal and answer the following questions:

1. Why are you alive?
   a) Define alive.
   b) Define what you do that shows you're alive.
   c) Define your outcome as if you were deceased. How you would want the world to know you?
   d) Define what is valuable in your life.

   **Example:** *A horse, land, your grandparents, your traditions.*

2. Take pride in life, for it is of the earth and so are you. What part of existence are you while you are on the earth? Choose one of the following:
   a) Are you the sky?
   b) Are you the ground?
   c) Are you the water?
   d) Are you the fire?
   e) Are you the stars?
   f) Are you the wind?
   g) Are you the spirit?

   After you have chosen one (and don't cheat—be honest—for it shows your sacred path), look at the definition. It will clarify who you are.

   **The sky**—the dreamer. One who anticipates and looks forward.. One who sees beyond simple reality and lives to make others happy. One who lives to bring new and exciting adventures to the earth.

   **The ground**—the worker. One who makes things happen. A designer, a builder, a laborer, a common retail merchant, a caretaker, a tender.

   **The water**—one of flow. One who counsels, a messenger, a child caretaker, a teacher, a traveler.

   **The fire**—the caretaker. One who sees, one who gives warmth, one who provides support, works with food, feeds the people.

   **The stars**—the storyteller. One who invents. A writer, a person of drama, an entertainer, an enlightener.

   **The wind**—the ancient one. One of Knowledge, lawyer, doctor, professor.

   **The spirit**—one of all. An artist. One who draws and paints, one of poetry, music, a gardener, a chef.

3. What is your Choice of existence?
   a) Human.
   b) Winged one, a bird.
   c) A four-legged animal. If so, what kind of animal?
   d) Swimmer.
   e) Crawly.

   As you choose one of these, you are describing your inner spirit guide. This is the one who enables you to see and understand what life is worth. When you choose the one that you know is right for you, you can begin to communicate with your four-legged or two-legged, your crawly or swimmer, or the human that could be your celestial guide—one of angelic form, an angel or a deva.

4. What is your favorite color?
   a) Red
   b) Orange
   c) Yellow
   d) Green
   e) Blue
   f) Purple
   g) Burgundy

   Choose one of these seven colors. It will describe your spirit walk. The lessons and medicines within the wheel share their values with you and show you how to follow your sacred path, the lessons you need to work on, which ones might be the hardest ones for you to understand. It will show you the medicines that will bring forth your life.

   > **Example:** *You've chosen yellow. Therefore, the word is Creativity. You are one who makes things happen. You are a talker. You are one who brings forth. Your lessons are those of following your Vision and being creative, applying Ceremony and Prayer to your life daily. (To understand the colors, look in the back of the book under Colors.)*

## PERSONAL NECK CLOTH

As human two-leggeds we have the need to feel comforted, secure about ourselves. The personal neck cloth is an article of clothing that has been worn for a long time by cowboys. Back in the 1800s it was worn by the Cavalry and it has been taken on by Native Americans and worn during their dancing time at powwows. The neck cloth keeps the throat chakra covered and it carries your personal medicine. It is very important that we express the thoughts that come from our mind. The neck cloth will also help you have Confidence in what you say.

**Tools:** *A piece of cloth the size of a normal bandanna, in any one of the following colors—white, light blue, light green or light pink; some cloth paints and a brush, if needed, or cloth paint pens (available at your local craft store); your smudge bowl and herbs; your journal and pen.*

Making a personal neck cloth is an empowering act. It is designed in Ceremony, so you will need to take your journal, open it to a clean page, and plan out your neck cloth. Look at the diagram and you will see that the top right corner is the East, the bottom right corner is the South, the bottom left corner is the West, and the top left corner is the North.

Start by selecting the color of your personal neck cloth: white if you were born in January, February, or March; red if born in April, May, or June; green if born in July, August, or September; blue if born in October, November, or December. Red is the symbol of the East, green the symbol of the South, blue the symbol of the West, and white is the symbol of the North.

# DECORATING YOUR NECK CLOTH

Your neck cloth can be as empowering and as fancy as you wish. It can be painted or stitched, you can attach rhinestones, or sew other objects onto it. I like to paint mine for I don't like to lose anything such as sequins or stitches. Make yours as simple or as complicated as you need.

1. Top right-hand corner—represents Spirit
   a) what is your favorite color?
   b) what is your favorite symbol-a square, a circle, a rectangle or a straight line?

   When you have chosen these two, draw your favorite symbol in your favorite color in the top right-hand corner.

2. Bottom right corner—South. Draw your emotions in black.
   a) acceptance
   b) disgust
   c) happiness
   d) sadness
   e) fear
   f) anger
   g) joy

   Put your way of expressing those emotions down in a symbol.

   *Example*: *Acceptance, little wavy lines for water. Disgust, a face with a tongue sticking out. Happy, a smiley face. Sad, an unhappy face. Fear, two big eyeballs. Anger, two eyeballs with teeth showing. Joy, two pine trees with a sun, moon and seven stars. You can make up your own symbols for the emotions.*

   On your cloth, paint your favorite emotion and paint the emotion you have the most trouble with.

3. The left bottom—the West.
   On a separate piece of paper:
   a) Draw a symbol for the human kingdom.
   b) Draw a symbol for the animal kingdom.
   c) Draw a symbol for the winged ones.
   d) draw a symbol for the swimmers
   e) draw a symbol for the crawlies

Now, choose one of these symbols to represent you and place it in black on the bottom left-hand corner of your cloth.

4. The top left-hand corner—the North. For the mind, you can choose from the following.
   a) If you have a personal Vision, draw that Vision in the most simple way.
   b) If you have a reoccurring dream, draw a symbol for that dream.
   c) If you have a lucky symbol, draw that symbol.

Place any of those symbols on your cloth to represent the brain/mental/soul section of the North.

When you have painted your symbols in each corner of the cloth, let the cloth dry, and it is ready to be worn. If you don't want to paint your cloth but just want to wear a bandanna, pick a bold colored cloth that corresponds to your birth month.

Always wear your neck cloth so that the point—the direction that you are working with—is showing, so that people can see it, as in the diagram.

**Example:** *If you are working with your emotions, tie the cloth so that the south corner is showing. Working with physicality, tie it with the west corner showing, and likewise when working with the spirit, you would have the east corner showing, or the North when working with the mind.*

You may choose to wear the neck cloth so that the point hangs down in the back, covering the back part of your heart. You would wear the cloth this way to protect your heart chakra.

Wear your neck cloth when you are not feeling well because of a cold, when you feel that you need personal Strength, when someone seems threatening to you, or when you are weak and afraid. Wear it any time you wish to be empowered by the medicine from the Rainbow Medicine Wheel. Wear it out for the public to see at dances or ceremonial events, on the night or day of the full moon, or at the solstices to celebrate the seasons.

Your personal neck cloth will bring you years of joy and empowerment. When you are not using your cloth, fold it and place it at your altar in your home, or at your medicine wheel inside your home, or keep it folded in a hope chest or an appropriate cedar box that will keep it safe.

Aho.

1.

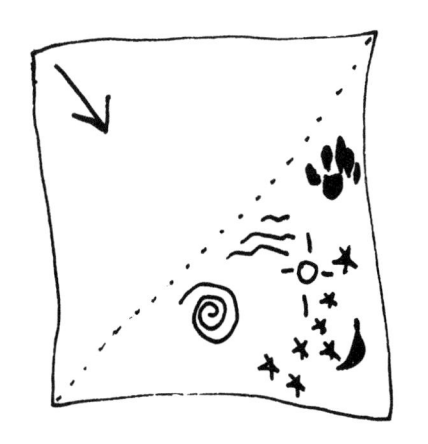

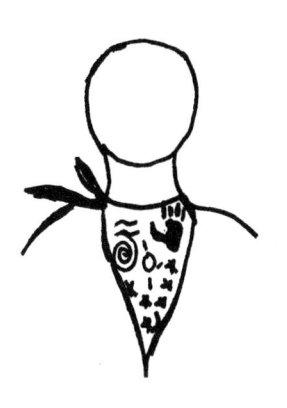

2.

3.

39

# 3 ◆ THE VOICE OF GRANDMOTHER/ GRANDFATHER WOLF

I breathe in and out. Before me I see the path, a snowy path, winding its way toward the mountain. I know that there is nothing easy about the North.

Each of us crosses through death; it is transformation. I so hope that each student understands, as they drop their robe (the Native American term for dying and leaving a physical carcass behind), that each and every spirit is alive in the spirit world.

I am surrounded by the night. The darkness is clear and stars glisten overhead. In front of me, the silent solitude of the mountains beckons. Come. Come to the Knowledge. That is the thought I hear.

"Yes, Granddaughter, come to us," I hear a familiar voice say. "Your Grandfather and I await you in the mountains. Hurry."

It is always good to be in the spirit world for I can leap and fly. I work my way high into the mountains and come to a place where there is a hole in the rocks. Morning is coming, dawn is at hand. I step through the hole in the rocks and before me the path becomes that of home. I can smell the wood, the fragrance of piñon, pine, hickory, and oak—the aroma of a campfire. I hurry along the path knowing that at any minute I will see my Grandmother and Grandfather Wolf. Now I can see the campfire, beyond the trees a ways. And there she is, hanging clothes on the line—the old wolf woman, my Grandmother Wolf herself. She looks up and waves at me, and I wave back.

"It's great to see you!" I shout.

"You, too! Hurry here. I have lots to tell you."

"I'm on my way! I have lots to ask."

From the side I am charged by Grandfather Wolf. His large arm reaches around me and hugs me tight. We race towards Grandmother.

"Hurry, Grandfather, keep up with me. You're doing good for an old one."

He runs quickly—outruns me even—and touches Grandmother before I do. He turns and smiles a toothless grin. His long braids are tied with red; his clothes are made of skin, and around his neck hangs a necklace with an intricate pattern. It is turquoise around the edges. Then in the center is a star-shaped circle of white, and in the center of that a circle of black, and in the middle of that is a burgundy star with a yellow star in the center. It is fringed in turquoise beads, with black and white, and black and turquoise, and loops of white beads at the bottom. The necklace itself is made of long bone beads with gold and silver beads and two pieces of turquoise on each side.

I touch it and say, "What a beautiful piece, Grandfather."

He smiles and says, "Yes, life is good. It is a good day."

Then he goes off towards the woodpile, singing, "Ya ho, hee haw. Ya haw, aho. Ya haw ne hay. Ye hay. Ha. Ho."

I love to hear him sing; his old withered voice carries the tune of the wind. Sometimes when I am getting to sleep, I hear his songs whistling through the pines. They are often on my mind.

Grandmother grabs me, hugs me, and gives me a kiss. I always loved to see the old woman with her beady, little eyes, toothless smile, and her chin touching her nose. Her beautiful white hair is braided perfectly. She smells of the campfire, sage and sweet grass; the scent of earth and fresh air is in her hair. I hold her, that tiny one, close to my heart. It is always a privilege to reach that place where her words guide my mind.

"So, you're on another adventure, Wolf. Sharing with the students the words of the sun and the moon and the seven stars."

"Yes, Grandmother. I want to speak to them about the Knowledge of the mind. It is hard, Grandmother, for they get caught up in the brain."

"Yes," she smiles. "They do that. They think the mind is the brain. There they miss a lot. It is yours to tell them differently, Granddaughter. It is yours to share with them truths—the Truth of your mother and father, the moon and the sun—the truths of the sacred circle, the Council of Wisdom, the Knowledge of the North, the seven stars, the sacred words of the sacred sisters."

I take a deep breath. "It is cold here, Grandmother, but I'm glad to be home."

"Yes, Wolf. Come sit with me in our house, and I will tell you of the mind. I will share with you words to give to those students and your assistant, to answer their questions."

We walk on the little path Grandfather has dug in the snow. Just beyond the house was the largest of all the Grand Mountains.

"Yes, Granddaughter, that is what I want to speak to you about. I want to share with you about the face of the Creator. Come in and sit down."

The cabin is sweet and small. Grandfather had built it, log by log, and between the logs is this beautiful mud that he packed from the river. The house is simple, one room and a fireplace. In the corner is the bed he made with his own hands. In the other corner is a fireplace he built with the rocks from the river. In front of the fireplace are the old rocking chairs and the handmade table that he put together for Grandmother long ago. He said that was before the sun and moon were made, before the stars cascaded and made the pathway to earth, before the Earth Mother brought her children forth. He made this chair a place where all could sit. He made this place, the table, the house, the place where we all played, where the bear cub learned, the dogs ran, the wolves sing their song, and the coyotes cut their teeth. Long before humans existed, Grandmother/Grandfather brought forth the sweetness of life in the hand-carved wood of the table that all could come to and sit at, and drink their tea.

"Sit here, Granddaughter. Sit here at the table your Grandfather has made."

I sit down and put my hands on the wood, and I can hear the stories. I can hear the songs of the universe, the whistle of the grand eagle. I can hear the Creator bringing forth laughter and the children. I hear life as we know it to be, through the palms of my hand. I sit there at the table wondering what Grandmother has to share with me now.

She walks over, steps on a stool, reaches up above the hearth on the fireplace, and opens up a rock door. She takes out a box, a beautiful pine box that is carved in criss-cross patterns. She sets it on the table before me, opens it, and takes out five little bottles, glass bottles. I am curious and want to touch them.

"Eh, eh. Don't do that, Granddaughter. Don't touch life. Don't be curious, for it might burn your fingers. Heh, heh," she laughs a sly, little laugh and looks at me with mystery in her eyes. "Here before you are the aromas. They are the smells of existence. From these tiny glass bottles come forth the essences of all."

I look at them sitting on the table. They are beautiful bottles. The first one is four inches tall, the second one three, the third one two, the fourth one, and the fifth one just a half inch high. One is clear glass; the others are burgundy, purple, blue, and green. Their tops are plugs—glass plugs—and the glass is all gold. The bottles are etched in gold circles with fancy designs spiraling around them.

I am still curious and reach out to touch them.

"No. No," Grandmother says. "Do not open the bottles. Haven't you heard of Pandora's box?"

She sits quietly, looking at the bottles. "I keep these here. I watch over them. It is in the North and the quiet of the snow, that the answers are. First, before life can be, it smells. It is before physicality that the essences come. It is from all that the essences are. I bring these bottles out in honor of all, for I wish to speak to you about the sacred medicine wheel. I think there is a great Mystery about what the North holds in store and I think that it is your time to walk with the White Wind."

She looks at me curiously.

"I remember him saying that, Grandmother. Dark Eyes called me the White Wind."

"Yes," she nods. "The White Wind is the North. It holds within it the keeper of Prayer, the sacredness of white, all that is pure and true."

"Grandmother Wolf, is it true there was a Buffalo Woman who walked on the earth?"

"Oh yes, dear, the White Buffalo Woman—her color is white. And there are also the White Owl Woman, the White Mare Woman, the White Eagle Woman, the White Wolf Woman, and the White Raven Woman. They are the ones with the stories of Beauty. They are the ones with the poetry of motion, they are the heartbeat—the seven sisters, the ones of sweetness, a place that we know as the Pleiades. They hold the secrets within their hearts, the stories of the broken heart, the stories of the fulfilled hearts, the stories of the sacred heart. They are the givers of cherish and Nurture. They are the teachers of Knowledge and Will. They are the home of the wolf."

As she speaks these words I hear the most beautiful music. It is being played on a cello. It is a haunting sound the cello plays, and I listen. The fire crackled and pops. The old cat, Thomas, stands up and stretches. He yawns and lies back down. I look through the window as the snow falls softly.

"It's amazing, Grandmother, how this place is so like the earth."

"Ah, yes, but different, Granddaughter. What did he say to you? What was he telling you?"

"Who, Dark Eyes?" I ask.

"Yes. He speaks. He speaks of that bottle," and she points to the blue bottle. "Within it is the breath of the Blue-Eyed Raven."

I sit very quiet. I hear my heart beat. The coldness of the floor seems to be filling up my body.

"I'm so cold, Grandmother."

"No! Don't think that." Her eyes come wide open. "Think of the fire, the warmth. Think of spring, of the memories."

I shake my head no. "It does no good, Grandmother. Tell me of the sacred wheel. Tell me why he said goodbye."

"Shhh." She puts her finger over her lips and rocks back and forth in her chair. She reaches out and takes the little blue bottle. "Everything is the sacred wheel. It is the oldest of all. The North, South, East and West—two sets of two—they are the sacred twins: the spirit and the body, the mind and the emotions. They are the four directions. They are the Song of the Raven. That is your memory. That is what you have come through the North gate for."

"Grandmother, is it true that you are not to cross out of the gates? Is it true that when you walk in the medicine wheel you only walk inside?"

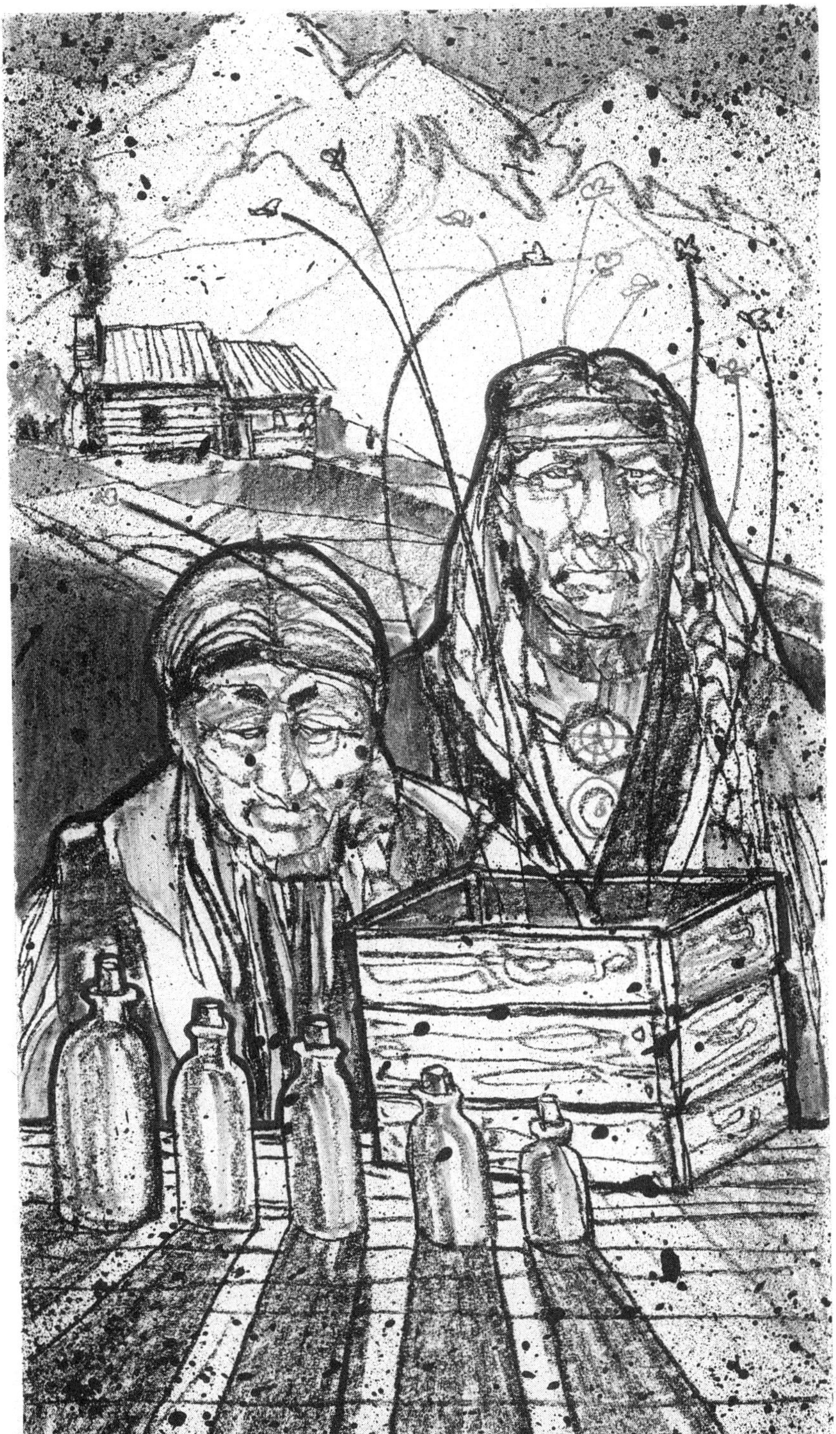

"On earth that is true, Granddaughter," she says. She scratches her head and gazes at the fire. She seems far away—very far away.

"Grandmother, what is it?"

"Oh, I was thinking of limits. I was thinking of the lightning storm within the brain. I was thinking of the day it all happened, the time when Mystery became known. You know?" She continues rocking to a gentle beat that I can hear. The beat of a drum echoes around the room.

"It's okay, Granddaughter. It's all okay. The time is almost here when all know. It is clear that you have brought the words, that you walk with the old ways and that you remember."

"Where is Dark Eyes going?" I ask.

"It is like the one who wants to know about the sacred wheel. He goes nowhere, for he is here," and she puts her hand over her heart, holds her hand out and touches my heart. "He is there, in you. He is the laughter. He is the joy. He is the South and you are the North. Everyone is either North, South, East, or West. They are from that circle and that time."

"Time. That's interesting, Grandmother," I say. "Time. They speak of time as if it is only man-made."

"They are right," she says. "Time is only man-made. Time—there is none. Time—there is some. Here, we have no time. Here, we have nothing but peace. Here we have the totality of Will. Here we are at the beginning point in the center of the wheel. The sacred spiral moves out from here. The motion of life is all around each one of us and it is known as existence. The levels are complex and each stone is the way. Each memory is the moment. Some are as old as the fire, and some are as young as a water droplet. He knows those things. You know those things."

"Hmm. That's interesting, Grandmother. He knows those things. I know those things. What about the sacred wheel? What has it called me home for this time?"

"It's simple. When they ask you, you must tell them what you smell."

She takes the tiny bottle, the blue one, and holds it up. She lifts the top, a dropper at the end of a lid, and she holds it to my nose. I can smell life. I can smell the desert.

"Yes, sage," she says. "It is sage. Breathe deep the oil of sage."

I breathe in deeply and I see the medicine wheel standing alone, on its own power. I see the red flag on the East gate. I see the green flag on the South gate, the blue flag on the West gate, and the white flag on the North gate. Entering through the East gate, I see a one-dimensional wheel lying on the ground, and I see the doorways, the gates.

"Smell," she says.

I smell the earth. I smell the power of sage.

"What is this about, Grandmother?" I ask.

"You will know, " she says with a tiny laugh. "It is all in the Song of the Blue-Eyed Raven. It is within your mind."

"I know that I am in the mind, the mental, the brain part of the medicine wheel. I know that, Grandmother. But these tiny bottles—they are so familiar."

She smiles a sweet grin. "Yes, they are, Granddaughter."

She gets up from her chair, goes over to a cabinet and opens it. She brings out another box, one made of dark wood. She sets the box on the table.

She says, "Close your eyes and breathe in and out seven times."

I breathe in and out, and while I am breathing, I hear the clinking of glass. I can't help it, I look a little, and she is opening the first bottle. It is clear glass. She takes a drop of the oil, puts it on top of the box, touches it to my nose, and closes the bottle. I finish my seventh breath and open my eyes. The box is open. It holds within it fireflies.

"They belong to the sun," she says, smiling.

The fireflies disappear.

"Long before the flower went to earth, where all the deep secrets hid, did dance the dust in the wind," she says. "Even as the golden, glittering grain, the fireflies are older than thee. They hold within them the story, the power of green and in this box I have the most precious...."

"Grandmother, does this box hold secrets, or is it teachings of the medicine wheel?"

"Oh, the medicine wheel. It is the safeness. It is the goodness of light. The medicine wheel is the place where one can endure. It is a comforting, loving place for it is pieces of the story—the rocks, the earth it sits on, the old pieces of limbs, the arms from the trees—that make the gates."

She reaches towards the box. Her little hands shake, but I can see the power of the wolf paws. "There is one you must see, the one who holds the secrets within the silk cloth—she, the queen of fireflies. She is the one you seek. You will grab the horse, and the memories of the North will speak to you."

She looks at me with a question in her eyes.

"Grandmother, do you want me to go somewhere? Is that what you're telling me?"

"Yes, Granddaughter. You are on the final ride of the circle. Those who study come to the medicine wheel. They listen to the rocks. The secrets are within the circles—the circles of sacredness within the sacred circle of the medicine wheel. Bridle the horse as you hear me sing now. Hurry. Go to the white horse. Follow the trail and find the queen of the fireflies."

"But Grandmother, it's winter. There are no fireflies in the winter. There are no lightning bugs this time of the year, Grandmother. They're not here."

"Oh, you will find them, and when you have found them, they are the Will. The face of Creator will smile on you and you will see the new moon, you will see beyond the full moon. You will remember when the earth's dark secrets are known to you. My blessings will be given to thee. Do you understand?

"You see, Granddaughter, humans came to the medicine wheel to learn the secret, the secret of the beat of the drum. It is the heartbeat, the sound of the flute; it is the sound of the spirit, the sound of the rattle. It is the sound of the bones. The sound of the bones is the sound of holy, of sacred. and the howl of the Wolf—it is the voice of Truth. Granddaughter, you see, there was a time when everything was eight. In the physical world you only see half of the Truth, so your circle has only four directions in it. But what is truly there is eight, because the back part of physical is spirit. It was in the movement of two circles that all has happened. There is not a day that two circles can become one. To understand that there are two sides—physical and spiritual—is Balance. That is the center of the medicine wheel. Wisdom is the North, for Wisdom is the facts and the knowing of the facts. It is so important that each human learn that there are two sides of one.

"Everyone thinks it is zero and one. Numbers tell the Truth. It is the circle that the one comes from and the one is you. Any person who tells Truth tells the story of Balance, the facts, the things that have been from the beginning." She gives her big, toothless grin.

"Grandmother, what are you up to?"

"Granddaughter, when you get to Will, you will have learned the lesson of inner peace and you will share it with all. It is time, for it is the new blue world. There are only two more worlds left, and the nightmare of death is over, and the dream of life is eternal. In the box I now hold is white silk and diamonds."

She lowers the box and I look in. I see a beautiful piece of white cloth that glistens with small diamonds that placed on the cloth in the form of snowflakes.

**I hear the howl of the wolf calling me back.**

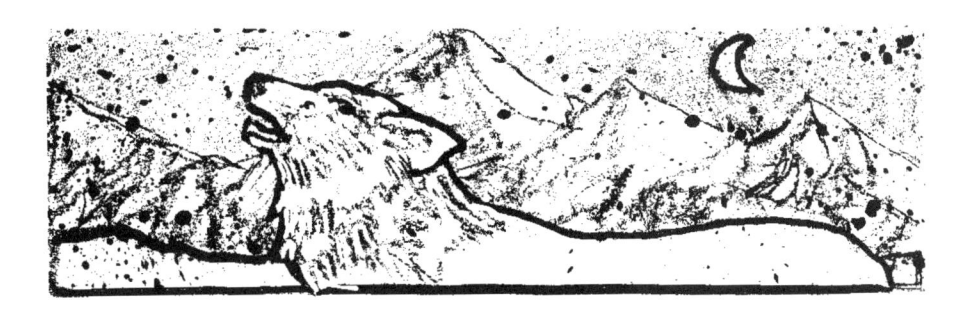

# THE RAINBOW MEDICINE WHEEL

In *Wolf Medicine* we are in the fourth section of the Rainbow Medicine Wheel. It is the section of the brain/mind, the mental understanding of the physical existence. Philosophy is old, older than human form, for thought is older than physicality. In our human existence we limit our life and we limit it gravely. We mimic each other. We take others at their word. We go to school and are taught how to act. Whether contemporary or traditional, the Native American circle of learning is a free form circle, which means that we are taught by the elements—the earth, the wind, the fire, the water, and by the sun and the moon and the stars. Each one of these is a precious teacher and a place within the medicine wheel.

The sun is the summer: the moon is the winter. The stars are medicines that we live with. These are the things I have learned from my elders, the stories my teachers have given me from the words of the wolf.

This medicine wheel is my Vision—the Vision of the sun and the moon and the seven stars. Look carefully and you will see two eights—four circles of life are the story of the medicine wheel. That is true—the medicines and the lessons. But there are more circles than that.

There is the center circle, which has seven stones in it. That is the elemental circle. That is Sweet Medicine. That is the first existence, the story older than humankind. It is the place where the cardinal directions are brought forth. It is the doorways, the gates, which the East, South, West, and North are. Within Sweet Medicine, you find the old stories of existence; how sound became, how the fire danced and how we can see.

There is a tiny circle in the center that is center itself, the point. That is Great Spirit. It is the diamond, the ultimate crystal, the point of perfection—Grandmother/Grandfather, Great Spirit/ Creator/ God/ All.

So in the medicine wheel there is the center. There is the circle around the center, which is the birth of the directions. There are the four directions. There are four sets of medicines and four sets of lessons. The four sets of medicines are four sets of seven. The four sets of lessons are four sets of seven. The center circle is a set of seven and the center itself is the point. There is a rhythm to the medicine wheel and that is one, four, seven. When you add those numbers together, one, four and seven, you get twelve. Add 1 and 2 together and you have 3. That is the sacred trinity within the medicine wheel. For it is Grandmother/Grandfather/Great Spirit/Creator, and the holiness of the hollow bone—one who lives a sacred life—that is brought forth from the medicine wheel.

Medicine wheels are full of Energy. They draw lightning, they bring forth the power of thunder. They encourage the snow beings to dance and the rain spirits to share. They enhance the Growth of the flowers and bring peace and harmony to everyone who lives in the vicinity of the wheel.

The wolf and the buffalo are the totems of the North. They are the guides and guardians that help you on the journey of the mind. The wolf is the sharp thoughts that help you hear the voice of Grandmother/Grandfather/Great Spirit. It can be a clear Knowing or voice that guides you in your everyday Choices. The buffalo is the feeling of soft guidance, the one that causes a need for advice or Prayer. The buffalo is the guidance that answers questions with a knowing. When you go to sleep knowing the answer, and wake up knowing the answer is the same as yesterday, this is the way of the buffalo. You know your Prayer is heard, and you know what to do in your daily life.

The wolf oversees the northern realm of the medicine wheel, for that is your pathway to Truth. The mouse accompanies the wolf as an assistant, bringing forth the Knowledge of scrutiny, paying attention, being aware. The buffalo is the spirit keeper of the North. It holds within it the opportunity of speaking, communicating, bringing forth Prayer, listening and receiving. Great Spirit is the infinite reality of the North. When you follow the pathway of Prayer, you are in the energy of Great Spirit. A trust in holiness and sacredness are the central beliefs of the Rainbow Medicine Wheel.

When we live our lives with Rainbow Medicine, we are walking the path of Grandfather/Grandmother Spirit. Trust is holiness. As we live with a clean mind that is sacred, we bring honor to our family and the Earth Mother. The center of the Rainbow Medicine Wheel is Great Spirit, which is being able to trust that all in life is good.

Aho.

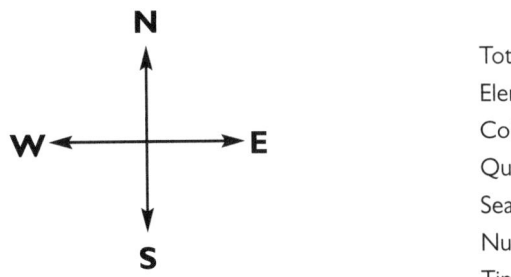

Totem: Wolf
Element: Air
Color: White
Quality: Knowledge
Season: Winter
Number: Seven
Time: Spirit time

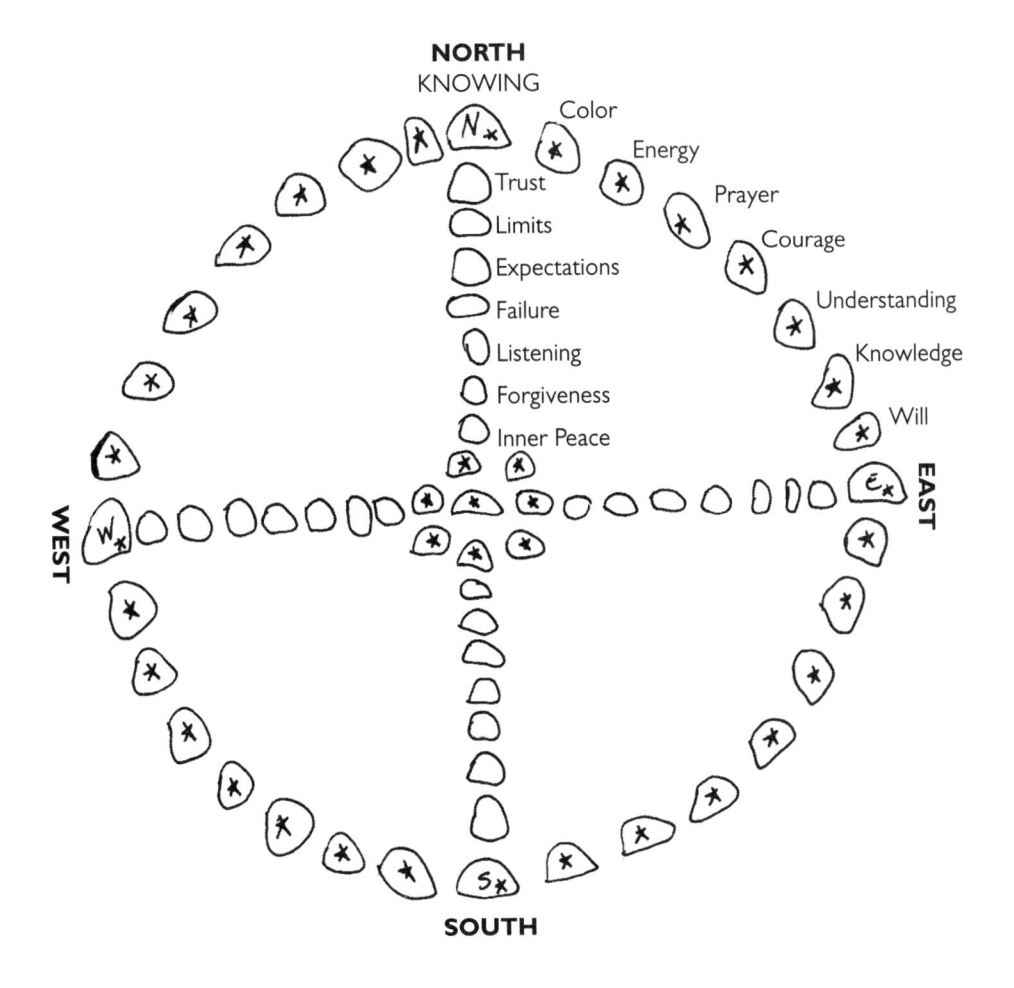

**NORTH**
KNOWING

Color
Energy
Trust
Prayer
Limits
Courage
Expectations
Failure
Understanding
Listening
Knowledge
Forgiveness
Will
Inner Peace

**WEST**

**EAST**

**SOUTH**

## The Rainbow Medicine Wheel

51

# 4 ◆ THE MAGICAL ONE— COLOR

I breathe in and out four times. Seven times I breathe. I feel a gentle, warm hand touch my shoulder. I look at his face, aged and withered. My Grandfather Wolf is strong. He has the wonderful look of the Native

American elder, though I see the wolf in his face, the power in his yellow eyes.

"That's right, Granddaughter. I am so proud of you today. Today you walk into the North. You leave here, at the base of the mountain, and you go in search of the magical one. You know him to be the Blue-Eyed Raven. He is the Truth teacher, one who holds magic in his song. Granddaughter, you will unite with him some day. And that day will bring forth the seven stars known as the seven truths, the sacred sisters, and all that is. For you and the magical one will walk as truth bearers. You will be simple, humble teachers who walk on the Earth Mother. Today I will give you a bundle. I will teach you the Ceremony of the Spirit Warrior, for in the bundle you will carry with you two talons of the eagle and two wolf teeth."

He stops and I see fear and worry in his face. "What is wrong, Grandfather? Speak to me."

I can smell the distant aroma of the oil that Grandmother placed on the tip of my nose. The fire is crackling. I look around the cabin. It is home to me, a place where I know I am safe. I have been safe here forever.

"There are those who are not awake. You live on the earth and you walk in the spirit world. You are from two places—a true shaman. One who guides the weary and strengthens the weak, but you walk equal to all, and that's what scares me. Will you know what to do when you die, Granddaughter?"

"Sure, Grandfather. I catch the black and white horse and I ride it across the Rainbow Bridge, and I take the path of stars as far as to here, where I will be home. And I'll meet him." I stop. I remembered that he is no more. The thought brings me to tears, and as one falls, it turns into a blue diamond and rolls across the floor. Then it turns into a star and shoots out the window, where it bursts into a million colored points of light in the sky.

"There will come a moment, Granddaughter, when you will understand Dark Eyes and you will not grieve, for there is no loss. Your love with him is strong and pure and brings forth hope. You have birthed hope. That is the Truth of the stars and you must remember that each one who walks on the earth can choose either destruction or opportunity.

"Now you must go. You are in search of the magical one, and the story along the way is the North. You will learn the medicines and become aware of the lessons."

He hands me a bundle that looks like a lizard. It feels funny to the touch.

"It is a lizard, Granddaughter. It is old and dry and has become a bag.

Inside is the Will. You must carry it now till the Spring thaw when Will touches enlightenment." He scatters dust in front of my face and I see trillions of colors, bright lights, and flashing points of color.

I awaken cold. The trees are dead, dead with winter. Everything was frozen and I am very cold. I take a deep breath and let out a sound—ooowwwww—which sounds like a wolf. I think for a moment of the loneliness of the wolf, how quiet its howl is, and how piercingly the sound cuts through the air.

I look ahead of me and there is a familiar place. An old woman comes toward me.

"Eh, get up from there, you old lazy wolf. Come here, come here," and she makes whistling sounds at me and mooches for me to come over.

"I'm not a wolf," I say. "I'm a person. My name is Wolf, but I'm not a wolf."

"Ah, you're a feisty wolf today, making those wolf sounds, swishing your tail. Come here. What are you doing down here all by yourself? You're supposed to be home. Come on with me. Come."

The old woman is fairly tall and round. A head scarf is tied around her hair. Her face is withered and old. She is dressed in a skirt of different kinds of fabric and a blouse made from cloths that are dirty and worn. She has an apron on, and no coat. Tiny sticks are tied on the bib of her apron.

"Get in here, come on."

I guess she thinks I'm a wolf. So I start following her.

"You better get on up to the house with me, you old wolf. You might think you know everything, 'cause you have walked on the earth many a year, but that doesn't give you no right to run away—now get in here!"

She opens the door of the old hut and I go in. She is not alone. There in the corner is someone I know, Old Stick Woman. Her scruffiness is unforgettable.

She looks at me and says, "I'd lay down there by that fire if I was you, and warm up. You know, you shouldn't be out there in that snow and ice. You could freeze to death even though you are a wolf." She winks. "That's a bad storm out there."

I hear the wind howling fiercely, banging up against the old hut. It is an interesting place made of sticks and various types of logs. They had made a mud paste and shoved bark, moss and grass in between each piece of wood. The hut is fairly large—a huge, round room. There is a fire in the center with the smoke spiraling out through the top. There are two beds—one on one side and one on the other—and old chairs made from tree limbs. Many herbs hang from the ceiling. On one side are beautiful tapestries, four of them, one for each of the four seasons. They are unique, for they are three-dimensional, made out of real objects—real stones, real twigs, real flower petals. They hang on the side of the hut where we are standing. A beautiful rug is on the floor. It looks like it was made from all different colored socks and it has beautiful buttons tied on it.

Old Stick Woman goes to the other side of the hut where a line is tied from one wall to the other. Close to the bed four dead and petrified chickens are tied to the line along with sticks and rocks, and feathers and wings from different birds. At the foot of the bed is a table made of tree limbs. The table has a stack of paperwork on it, and some tin cans. A pole that leans up against it has a crystal on the top. The crystal is tied on with rawhide.

Old Stick Woman sits on the bed. "I don't know what you need that old wolf for. That old thing is probably infested with fleas and ticks, anyhow." She lies down and pulls the blanket up over her head. "I just don't understand," she mumbles some more words.

"Don't pay that old thing any mind," says Grandmother Twigs. "I'll fix you something to eat. Why are you looking at me like that, Wolf? You look as if you don't know me. I wish you could talk sometimes. I wish you could speak to Grandmother Twigs. I just wish sometimes that you could talk and tell me of all the wonders you see on the path out there."

"Oh, wonders! You don't need to hear any wonders, you old woman," growls Old Stick Woman from beneath the covers. "I've told you about those people in town. I've told you so many times. You're so lucky Mom never let you go and live there. You know, being a daughter of Mother Nature, it looks to me like you'd understand. Now hush up."

I hold the bundle and wonder why they can't see who I am.

"They don't need to see," the bundle says. I hear the voice clearly. "They don't need to see. You need to know them and listen to their pain and to their Strength."

"You know, I've heard enough pain from Old Stick Woman. I saw enough to last me for a long time a ways ago," I say. "Here I am, talking to a bundle, anyhow. Who are you?"

"I'm Dreaming Lizard. I am the sacred color bundle. I hold within my eyes the memories of the colors, and tonight they will dance and you will hear and share their words."

Grandmother Twigs brings me over some food, and I eat and drink the fresh water she pours from the clay pot. I curl up at the fire as a wolf. The old one strokes my hair.

"You've been a good pathfinder for me. You've been a way of showing me life. You run into the woods and fight the most fierce and dark fears of my mind."

"It ain't your mind," Old Stick Woman says. "It's just your brain from drinking too much of that peach tea you drink. You don't have no fears. You've got no reason to be afraid. You're just twigs anyhow." Old Stick Woman laughs. "That's a good name Mom gave you, Twigs."

"You had better hush up, Old Stick Woman," Twigs says. "I could send you back out there to your place at the edge of town where nobody wants you anyhow. I could put you out there where nobody cares about you 'cause you're crazy."

"I'm crazy!" Old Stick Woman sits straight up in the bed and glares at her sister. "I ain't crazy. I ain't the one who's talking to a darned old wolf. You think that old wolf can talk back? That old wolf doesn't know nothin', and if it did, it'd probably talk about some way of living that you couldn't understand anyhow 'cause you ain't never seen no way of living, you old battle axe."

"Don't you be calling me those names," Twig says. "I don't need your names. I'm not that way. I've lived a quiet life. I can't help it that I speak for the spirit. You're the one who doesn't know anything. I can't help it that your purpose is just to be a lightning storm."

Oh, great. I guess I'm living inside a human's head somewhere. I listen to these two old women go at it for hours and I can tell that one of them is truly thoughts and the other one is all feelings. They speak of their angers and their fears. They speak of their worries and their troubles. They speak of how bad people are and they argue for most of the night. Finally, Old Stick Woman goes to sleep and Twigs is petting me, pulling on her wool socks and her nightgown and brushing out her hair. She mumbles something about mental illness. She mumbles about the frailties of human existence and wanders off to bed and to sleep.

I shake the lizard bag and ask if it can hear me, but there is no sound—just an old dried up lizard. I pull up a rocking chair. As my spirit, I sit in the chair while I see myself, the wolf, on the floor. I sit there rocking by the roaring fire and there before me is a large wooden door.

"Open the door," I hear the lizard say.

I open the door and there in the doorway stands a beautiful warrior. He is strong, a Native American warrior. He has long black braids. A string of feathers hangs from the left side of his hair down the front of his body. The feathers—hawk, eagle, blue jay, magpie, cardinal, oriole, flicker, raven,

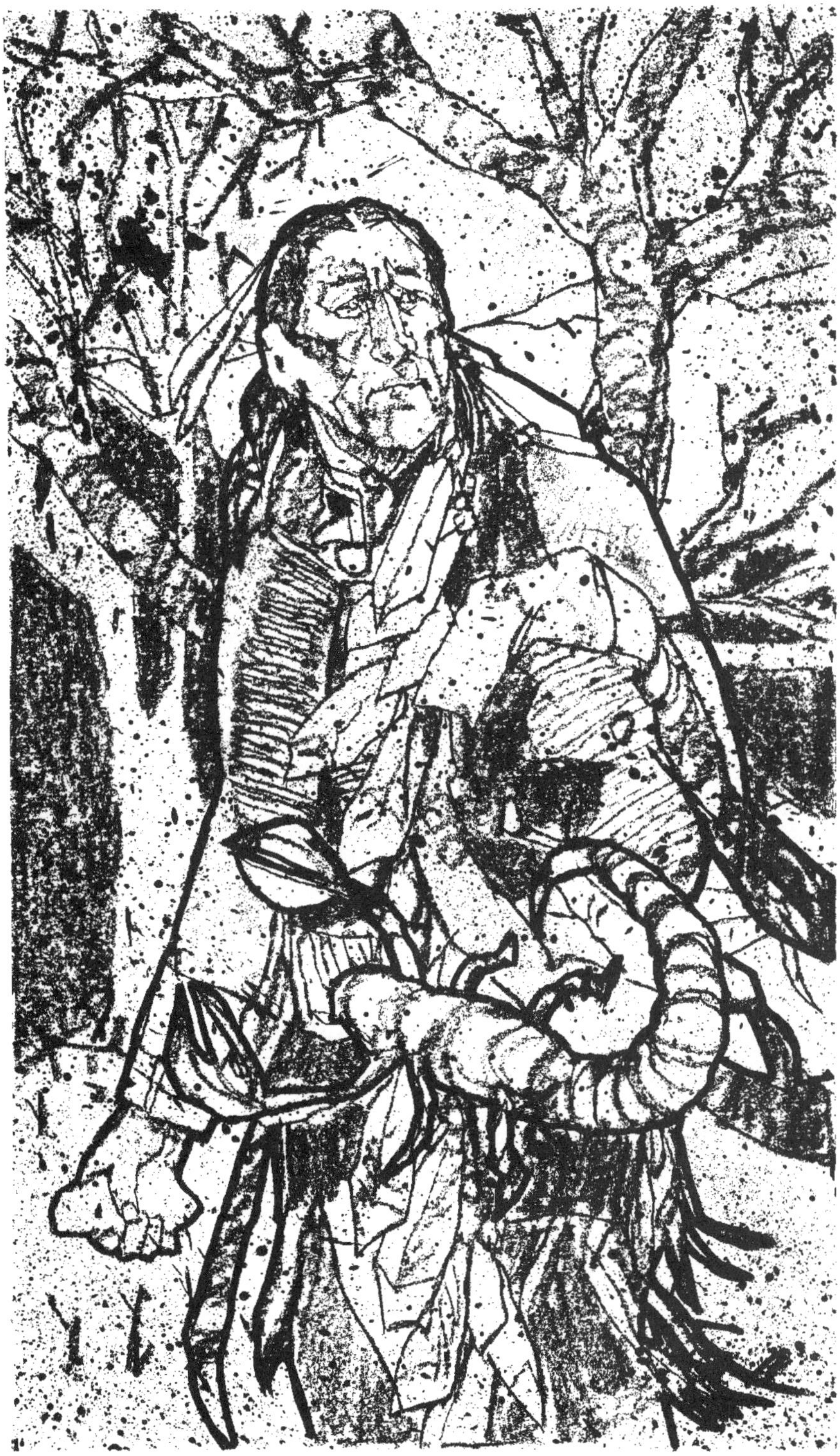

crow—are all beautifully attached to beads, and they reach all the way to the floor. I notice the beads are round balls. There is a red one, an orange one, a yellow one, a green, a blue, a purple, and a burgundy one.

"Good evening, Wolf. I am the Spirit Warrior. I hold in my hand a gift for you from Great Spirit." He holds out his hand and in it is a white wolf paw. I look at it.

"Where did you get that?"

"It is yours. You must take it now, for you will walk the way of the North."

I take hold of the wolf paw. It becomes my hand, my left hand.

"You must remember that you are of the mind. The mind is the voice of the brain. The brain is the lightning storm. It is the space in the cells where Knowledge is birthed. Look in your paw."

I turn my hand over and there are my seven stars.

"Yes, those are the teachings of the North. They are your fourth set of stars. You will come to understand Color and Energy, Prayer and Courage, Understanding, Knowledge, and Will. You will be tested by the lessons. Understand the lesson of limits. It will be the one that reveals the secrets of the distance between you and Dark Eyes. Remember that marriage will be a Choice. The door is open for you and your eternal life is rich and full, for your marriage will be strong. As the time comes on earth when your hair turns white at the temples, you will walk with the Blue-Eyes and gaze upon the Grand mountains and see through the window the soul and face of Color. You will understand creation and, through the great voices, learn the ways of your mother. Do not mourn ever, for death is simply a stone across the river. She is well and you are well. You must dance that walk and carry with you the throat cloth, the one that Grandmother Wolf has given you. When you stand in the face of Great Spirit and walk with the magical one, place the cloth around your neck and listen to the song of Sweet Medicine."

The fire shimmers and I see green and blue. The spirit disappears and I sleep.

I awaken to Old Stick Woman shaking me. "Wake up, there. See, I knew you wasn't a wolf. I know you. I remember you from when you came to see me," Old Stick Woman says, glaring at me. She pulls over a chair and sits down. "Now you sit up here and you listen to me. I'm going to tell you something right now. This here is my sister, Twigs. I keep her safe here in the woods, where they won't get her. You understand that?" She reaches in her apron. pulls out a pouch, and puts some chewing tobacco in her mouth. She starts chomping it around; she doesn't have very many teeth. but she mulls it around good.

"Yeah. Yeah, you remember me, don't you?"

I look at her and say, "How could I forget you? That night in your lodge was very scary. I still don't understand why you had those pumpkin heads out there on poles."

"Well, don't you be bothering about that. You probably wouldn't know nothin' about it—you're like the rest of them people out there. Yeah. Yeah, I was in town the other day and I saw those kids wearing black. You know, they're sad. Them kids are sad. And I'm not talking about an emotion, either. I'm talking about what people do to them. Them kids are clever. They're fox medicine, them kids are. But the old lizard is watching. Yeah, that pouch you've got there that you're hanging onto that your Grandmother/Grandfather gave you. You're gonna see here, because you're in the realm in the North. You're in this mental plane." She spits some tobacco in the fireplace. "You're going to teach people about how mean they are. 'Cause meanness, heh, heh, heh," she laughs a wicked old laugh, "meanness is mental illness. Yeah, those kids wear black because the parents aren't listening. They just judge them and the kids want to show them that. A kid will go far out to show you something. It's like a scorpion. Yeah, a black one."

Her eyes are flat and dull. Her hair is all scraggly and has come out from the sides and is hanging down around her face, white and wispy. She has pieces of lint and moss and some sticks hanging in the back of it, where it is all gobbed together and braided and tangled up.

"Hey, don't be looking at me like that. You ain't got no reason to be studying me," she says with a growl. "You better be listening, because you're going to be leaving here pretty soon and you're going to go out there. And they're out there waiting, those spirits, the snabbers. That's what they are, they're snabbers. They're thoughts that engulf you. The reason that you have come here is no surprise to me, Wolf. You do like to be called Wolf, don't you? You were chosen, as any elder would be, to tell the story of the soul. Do you think you can do that? What do you tell them when they ask you where their lost soul is? Many have come before you and couldn't. What are you going to say, huh?"

She takes another pinch of tobacco.

"You know, you'd break my sister's heart if I was to wake her up and she'd see you are just a mere mortal. She has great faith in you, that wolf laying there. You been with her a long time, walking with us as an old wolf.

Now I'm going to show you something. I'm going to teach you about a lesson."

She gets up and shuffles over to a cabinet, opens the door, and there is a can sitting there. It has a lid on it. She gets that can out and shuffles back over and sits down.

"Well, I don't care if it's 'cause they got a pistol, or it's 'cause they got some chewing tobacco that they ought not have in school, or that music, or they're wearing black, or whatever they're doing, they're just misunderstood. And they might even have a malfunctioning brain. You know, you got that brain in your physical body and it's like a lightning and thunderstorm. That's what its like, yeah." She spits again in the fireplace and wipes her hand across her mouth.

"You got to listen to this lesson. I'm going to show you something."

She opens the can and I see two kind of black wriggly things coming out the top. They look like the pinchers on a lobster.

She says, "Look here. Look here in this can," and she shoves it up in my face. I look in and draw back quickly. There is a scorpion in there.

"Yeah. That's a scorpion. That's a lesson. And you know what? It's deadly." She puts the lid back on. "It's a lesson of trust. That's what's taking them all. Them snabbers out there, they're scorpions—they're the lesson of trust. One thing that humans are killing themselves with is a lack of trust. And how can you blame them when people are tearing each other up like they do in this life? And you thought when you walked in the spirit world it all disappears? It ain't disappearing anywhere. You're being followed. You'll be followed into eternity with your evilness, if that's what you choose to call it. Everybody wants to run from everything and blame somebody. It's a simple thing—chemistry. It's lightning and thunder. I been studying them people. They don't think I know nothin'. Well, I've been reading. I been reading longer than they've been living. I been reading people. And I been watching.

"They blamed me when I was young. They said I was the reason the families fell apart. They called me a witch. Everybody got these words they like to call people," she says, a real intense look in her eye. "Them words don't do you no good. You've blamed me and put me out on the edge of the city. You can turn to the purty little girls with the fancy chests they got and you can say they're the reason. But their sickness is a reason. And sickness is the breath of the snabbers. It's the way of the scorpion. And all it is, is a lack of trust. You see, let me tell you something about trust. It slips in on you in the dark, like a scorpion, and its sting is fatal, 'cause once you can't trust, it's over. You understand that?" She pitches the can into my lap and I cringe.

"Oh, my God, please don't let that lid come open."

"That's right. Pray that you don't lose your trust in your faith. Because if you do, you're done for. You know it?"

I nod my head and feel my stomach do a double flip.

"Yeah, I know it. I know it real well because when I was on earth I experienced it about as bad as one human can take it. And I had friends who were children of abuse."

I look down at the floor and the fear rushes over me. I want to throw the can in the fire. I feel the darkness and the heat of being shut in that dark place of my childhood. I gasp and say a silent Prayer. "Grandfather, get me out of here. This old woman, she's right. We want to say she's crazy and we want to reject what she says, but she's right and I don't want any part of this."

"Eh, well, you ain't getting away right now 'cause you got to listen. Them snabbers, they take. They're shadow dancers. This here scorpion, he's a shadow chaser. They got to stay in the dark, where it's cool. They can't live in the sun. They die when they come out in the sun. You see trust, it can't live in the shadows. It has no shadows. It has no darkness, it is only light. But you've got to listen to the shadow dancers. They are only feeding—not doing anything else but feeding. They just feed in the dark."

She looks in the fire and gets quiet. I set the can down on the floor.

"What's next?" I say.

"Here, let me show you." She takes the can and opens it. The scorpion crawls out on her arm and sits there.

Oh, I was filled with fear! It was a deadly, eight-inch, black scorpion from Africa. She puts the can in front of her, and it goes back in.

"He's not hungry. He's afraid of that fire. It's too much light and heat. But I knows it, 'cause I've lived it. I'm here, Old Stick Woman that lives out here on the edge. I'm here to tell you. You'd better be careful. 'Cause when you lose your trust, then you are jeopardizing everybody. You see, I know 'cause I got some medicine, Color, in me. I hold onto my spirit Knowledge. It's my job to teach them childrens that they're not bad. You're going to go, Wolf, and you're going to be out there in it. The Energy is coming. You must know about the scorpion."

She flips me over a piece of resin. It was a pretty good-sized piece, about three inches, and inside of it is a baby scorpion.

"See, he's been frozen there in time. That's what mental illness is, it's a freezing of the mind. It's a sad thing that no one wants to listen. They want to pretend, call people crazy like your mom—Crazy Helen, you know? She was a lot like me, 'cause she was a scorpion."

She takes the can, gets up, and wobbles back over to the cabinet. She puts the can back and walks on over towards her bed.

"I have nothing to say to you now. Get out of here. When the sun rises, you go, 'cause you can walk in the sunlight. What about the shadow dancer who can't?"

She gets in her bed and pulls the covers up over her. I sit there looking at the fire, holding the lizard bag, wondering where I will go. I have no fear of scorpions because I was raised by one. Just because something is deadly and lives in the darkness, it does not have the ability to shake my trust. I fear not the snabbers.

**I hear the howl of the wolf calling me back.**

## COLOR TEACHINGS—LIZARD MEDICINE

We are human, but that is a small part of what we are. We are spirit, and that is all of what we are. The teaching of color is a simple statement. You have quality and substance. You have a viewpoint and an attitude. You are a tone. You have appearance. You are constantly evolving. Color brings forth the opportunity for each one of those things to happen.

You can look at your life as a magical presence or you can see it as a human existence. You can live it like everybody else or you can be unique. When you work with your personal qualities—your smile, for example, or your personality—you are setting the base point for yourself. The base point is what you build everything from.

The color red is your intensity. The color orange is your substance. Your yellow is your viewpoint, and your green is your attitude. Blue is your tone, purple is your appearance, and burgundy is your evolvement. When you look at yourself, you are skin tone, you are pigment, you are hue, and you are light reflection.

The medicine of the lizard speaks about being careful of the illusions. It tells us that we have to watch out because we will know our dreams. When you put color in your life and you look at your qualities, you are the eyes of the lizard.

As a medicine word Color is all energy, all colors. When you see a color it has its teaching and Power. Each color in humankind has a spirit and story. If there is no Color, there is no life, no Energy, no spirit. The Lizard is the Color totem. It teaches the reality of dreams and Vision. It is the symbol and teaching of achievement and completion. The lizard is often hidden from the eye of the seeker, as Color is not noticed to its fullest.

Color shows us the material and spiritual side of all. There is Color in all of physical existence. You have your total Power when you see and use Color in your life. The brain gives us the ability to see Color, and the mind tells us of the feeling behind the Color.

When you are in a slump or are scared, Color is the medicine to apply. Color heals in all circumstances. Every lesson in life can be changed if you see the lesson in a different Color. Color gives definition to life.

Aho.

## THE LESSON OF TRUST— SCORPION MEDICINE

Trust is one of the lessons in life that makes or breaks us. As we live life, we humans base each move on our ability to think. Human beings must trust, for thoughts need a foundation. As a small child, a human being learns by watching. Trust is the action that takes place when we learn as children. Trust is dependence, children would starve if the parent or someone didn't feed them. The lesson of trust usually comes when we face different teachings in our youth and adulthood. Any time we are confronted by a teaching that is different from our own, we are interacting with trust.

When trust is broken, a person is affected strongly, maybe even forever. The part of trust that is the hardest part to learn is to accept that all things and people are different. When you see all the facets of life, you have learned the lesson of trust. When your thoughts are changed, you look at matters in a different way. This is trust: you are trusting a new way of thinking.

The lesson of trust is having the ability to roll with the punches. The lesson of trust is to remember that you can apply the medicine of Choice and Change your thinking to achieve any goal.

Color treats the lesson of trust. Sunshine is Color, green is Color and a smile is bright yellow and is Color. When you apply Color to the lesson, you are acting in trust. When you are in pain due to a lack of trust or your trust has been broken, you need to think of the Power of Color, all the colors.

The totem for the lesson of trust is the scorpion. Trust has a sting that is deadly if you base your needs on trust and cannot flow or go with the lesson. The dark side of trust is blame. When we lose trust, we as humans cast blame. Applying Color to this dark side will bring light to the fact that you have Choice. In learning the lesson of trust we must be in check always, knowing that all is spirit and all is good. It is always a good day to be alive! Aho!

## CEREMONY OF THE SPIRIT WARRIOR

**Tools:** *Seven black candles, and seven colored candles—red, orange, yellow, green, blue, purple, and burgundy; candle holders that will keep the candles from setting the ground on fire (you can buy these at your local store); journal and pen; yellow cornmeal; smudge bowl and herbs; wooden matches.*

A spirit warrior is one you can call upon, who will help you apply Color to the lesson of trust. Color is brightness; it is sunlight; it is bold. In the lodge I like to use red, orange, yellow, green, blue, purple, burgundy in their true form—the same colors as in a package of crayons you might buy.

The Spirit Warrior is in your mind. It speaks from your spirit, from existence, from Grandfather/Grandmother/Great Spirit. It shows you that you have lizard medicine, that you have Color. Remember that the scorpion is a most powerful and deadly creature. It strikes fast and causes great pain, as does a loss of trust. When we lose our trust, we call upon the Spirit Warrior to assist us in going out and getting the help we need.

Some people believe that Ceremony is bad—dark and evil. Ceremony is actually Prayer, and it is done in a circle because a circle is the strongest symbol of Energy that there is. As we work with this symbol, we bring forth Healing from the Spirit Warrior, which is our inner self coming forth to give us a message from Great Spirit. In the medicines of Color we can reach out and open ourselves to the purest form of bright light. We do not have to be shadow dancers, hiding within ourselves. We can allow ourselves to stand up in the pureness of Color.

To perform the Ceremony, you need to find a spot where there is dirt or sand that you can draw in. Pick a place that is quiet and where no one can disturb you, to do the Ceremony of the Spirit Warrior. You could use your back yard or patio by pouring plant potting soil on a tarp or on the ground, about two inches (5cm) thick, so you can draw in it.

When you're ready to begin, draw a circle in the dirt. Then draw a line through the center, putting about seven inches (17.5cm) of the line above the circle and seven inches below it. Fill the right-hand side of the circle with yellow cornmeal, as if you are painting that half of the circle yellow. Make sure that the cornmeal is about a half an inch to an inch (1.25 to 2.5cm) thick. Now place your candles for the lizard (the color ones) in the yellow cornmeal. Start at the top with the red candle and move to the bottom of the circle, ending up with burgundy.

On the left side, the dark side of the wheel, put the black candles. It is important to remember that black is the symbol of wholeness and transformation. It also has the power to repel negative energies.

Take out your journal and write the Ceremony of Spirit Warrior:

1. Write the word "Scorpion." Beneath it, make a list of your pains, hurts, anguish, disappointments, and disagreements, from 1 to 7, listing the seven most important negatives you have in your life.

> **Example:** *#1—don't understand myself. #2—alienated by other people. #3—suffered from divorce, etc.*

After you have listed all seven, look back at them, think about them, and make sure they are the things that cause you the most pain, that cause you the most despair in your life today.

2. Place the word "Lizard." Beneath it, list your desires, your strengths, your greatest strong points in your daily life, starting with 1 and going to 7. List things that make you happy, things that give you solid support.

> **Example:** *#1—full of desire. #2—full of joy. #3—looking forward to my new education. #4—excited about the birth of a child.*

When you have listed all seven, look back and make sure that they are the strongest points of joy and happiness that you have in your life.

3. Now in your journal take each one of the seven Scorpion listings and write about how it came to pass—who caused it, what is the reason for it happening, and how it has affected your life in a negative way. Do that for each example.

4. Now take the seven things that you wrote down under Lizard—those that

have to do with the joyful things in your life. Write about how they happened, how did you gain your joy, how did you get your Strength, who is your joy, what is your Strength, etc.

5. When you have finished, compare the two lists. See if your lizard list is the one where you have placed a lot of emphasis upon yourself—*you* seek out your joy, *you* bring yourself happiness, *you* open the doorways to understandings, *you* experience wonderful places and experiences in nature and with wildlife. Then see if, in the Scorpion section, you have placed a lot of blame—other people have hurt you, other people caused things, other people are the ones who make life hard, other people are killing the earth.

6. Now that you have compared the two lists, it is time to go to the Ceremony. The first step is to light your color candles, starting with red. Look back over your list and reflect on what the red candle is about. (You'll find a description of each color in the back of the book.) Continue lighting your candles—orange, yellow, green, blue, purple, and burgundy.

Then look at the Scorpion side and ask yourself whether, if you applied a color to one of the black candles, it would make a difference. List in your journal the #1 black candle and what it is about. Then choose a color, take a wooden match, put it in the fire, and light the black candle from the medicine of the color.

Continue lighting your black candles, choosing a color candle that is appropriate for dealing with the Scorpion situation. Then, going through your Scorpion side of the list, write yourself notes on how you are going to Change the blackness, the darkness, the emptiness in your life.

> **Example:** *#1—do not like living, want to die—lit by the #1 medicine candle. Going to apply hope and see more positive actions in my life.*

7. When you are done, let the candles burn for a while. Read back through your list and see what it is going to take for you to be able to trust the colors. It would be a good idea to make some notes in the places where you have blamed others. This is an area in which you will need to seek out the advice of an elder (maybe a family member who is older and wiser, a spiritual leader, a spiritual teacher, a psychologist who specializes in family counseling, or a psychiatrist who specializes in family therapy).

Then, each day, at the same time for the next seven days, come back to the circle of the warriors, light your candles, and see how you are doing. You should get to a time where there is nothing to say with your black candles. Then you will light them all from the light of each color until you feel you have no weaknesses in your trust areas, until you feel you have no darkness in your life. When that has happened, remove the seven black candles and put one white candle in their place, meaning that the Ceremony of the Spirit Warrior is in Balance.

It is a good idea to leave your candles set up for a full seven days, and to let the Ceremony can go untouched. If that is not possible, then you will need to pick your candles up starting with the last one you put down, put them away, and bring them back daily as you do your Ceremony. Keep your journal entry very clear and do plenty of writing. If you have trouble with writing, use a tape recorder and tape your notes so that you can read or listen to yourself as you bring your Growth about.

As you work with scorpion medicine, you will come into the fullness of trust, learning that to trust you must have assurance, you must have sureness, optimism, reliability, safekeeping, Responsibility, and belief. To learn the lesson of trust you need to stand whole in yourself and answer the questions that made the negativity happen—do not blame others, do not blame situations. Go to the core of the matter.

Aho.

## COLOR MEDICINE BUNDLE

This bundle holds within it your color medicine strips, made from cloth, that bring forth your sacred Knowledge of self.

**Tools:** *A piece of red cloth, 12 inches (30cm) square, or a piece of deer skin, elk skin, or buffalo skin; a piece of white cord to tie it with if it is cloth, or a piece of leather cut in a strip ¼ inch (6mm) wide by 34 inches (85cm) long, if it is skin; seven strips of cloth cut ½ inch (12mm) wide by 34 inches (85cm) long—one red, one orange, one yellow, one green, one blue, one purple, and one burgundy; your journal and your pen; smudge bowl and sage.*

In your color medicine bundle, you will keep strips of color that represent your medicine. The medicine from the North is Color, Energy, Prayer, Courage, Understanding, Knowledge, and Will. Throughout this book you will be working with different words that help you understand your mental state.

To build your bundle, place your piece of cloth or skin flat down on the ground or on the table where you are working. Take the color strips and lay them out in front of you. The red one is the symbol of excellence. The orange one is the symbol of quality. The yellow one is a symbol of superiority. The green one is the symbol of personal action. The blue one symbolizes accomplishments, the purple one, attainment. The burgundy one is the symbol of achievement.

Look at these colors and at the medicines that connect with them. The medicine of Color brings about excellence. The medicine of Energy brings about quality. The medicine of Prayer brings superiority. The medicine of Courage brings forth personal action. The medicine of Understanding brings forth accomplishments. The medicine of Knowledge brings forth attainment. The medicine of Will brings forth achievement.

Take your journal out and list the seven words:

**1. Red**—write down the things that you are excellent at, the things that you have no doubt that you are absolutely great at.

**Example:** *Sewing, working on a car, playing a guitar, cooking.*

**2. Orange**—write down the things that represent quality to you.

**Example:** *The beauty of your hair or teeth or eyes, the beauty of the day, the sky.*

List the things that represent quality in your life.

**3. Yellow**—list those things in your life that show your superiority.

**Example:** *Degrees attained; a grade point of 3.8; a good marriage; wonderful children; a good, reliable, loyal pet; a Vision from Grandmother/Grandfather/Great Spirit/Creator/God.*

**4. Green**—List the action you will apply. Whether you are working with life problems or just want to have good actions in your daily life, you need to know the action to apply in your life. This can be a Choice of the medicine words:

Color—what color will you apply to your life to make a Change: red, orange, yellow, green, blue, purple, burgundy. Apply the words that are in the back of the book under Colors as the actions you will take.

**Example:** *Red—Confidence, Strength, Nurture, Color, Accountability. These are the words you would use to take action.*

**5. Blue**—List your accomplishments.

**Example:** *Have a job, I'm responsible and take care of myself; my health is good; I have a spiritual connection with Grandmother/ Grandfather/Great Spirit/Creator/ God; I have friends in my life. ( I once had a student who collected buttons, and she couldn't find any accomplishment in her life other than that she collected buttons. She had several generations of buttons and planned to pass them on to her little niece who was interested in buttons. This gave her a feeling of accomplishment. It was a place from which we could build and through which I could begin to show her her worth.)*

List any accomplishments that are valuable to you.

**6. Purple**—List your attainments.

**Example**: *Your room, your rental property, the home you own, your clothes, your life, degrees, money.*

When you are listing your attainments, understand that ownership teaches value. Understand that attaining something in one area is proof that you are able to attain in other areas as well.

**7. Burgundy**—List the things that you have achieved.

**Example:** *Your life; your mental health; your health in general; your marriage; your children; your job; your thoughts; your relationships.*

When you have finished listing these things, go back and write about them. Write about the adventures you have had in each subject. It is good to look at the stories in your daily life. By doing that, you can see patterns of experience and the Choices you have made. You can see where you have been in denial or where others have been in charge in your life. You can see where you have weak spots or need to take action and apply the medicines in your life. By writing in your journal you can tell where you are learning lessons and understand the need to learn more of the lesson. It helps to correct feelings of guilt and brings forth Strength in your life.

Close your journal and hold up the color strips, remembering what they mean. Place the strips on the bundle cloth. Take the right corner of the cloth and fold it to the left. Take the left corner of the cloth and fold it to the right. Take the bottom and roll it up over the top. Then wrap the bundle well with the cord and tie it.

# CEREMONY OF THE MEDICINE BUNDLE

Keep the Medicine Bundle by your bed, under your pillow, or at your altar so that you see it every day. On Sunday, take the bundle and go on an adventure, for the bundle speaks to you of your magic. It speaks to you of the Color in your life.

To set out on the quest of the bundle, go to a sacred place and find a stick. It needs to be three feet (1m) tall or taller. The stick represents your path, the road that you are on and how you feel about your path. It represents your existence and the worries or sicknesses, lessons or medicines you have in your life at the moment.

I like to call the stick a teaching stick. It speaks to me of the matters I'm working on in my personal life currently. I take it to the Rainbow Medicine Wheel at the lodge. In the bundle I keep the color cloth I will need to attach to the stick to represent thoughts, medicines, and lessons I'm working on.

I make a list of the actions I want to think about and be in Prayer with, and then I pick the color of cloth I want to work with and tie it to the stick. I place the stick at the wheel where the wind can blow the colors, and I see the color strips and think of the needs I have connected to each color.

In your journal make a list of any or all of the following you want to work with and tie a strip of color on your stick.
1. Worries you have—select a color for each worry.
2. Problems—do the same.
3. Medicines you need to apply to your life. Look in the back of the book and see the words and their color—do the same.
4. Lessons you are learning. Look in the back of the book and pick from the lesson words. Do the same.
5. Sicknesses—do the same.

**Example**: *I tie a red strip on for the worry over money. I then know I will use Confidence and Color to treat this worry. I tie a green strip on the stick for the Growth I will need to solve the problem of money. I know I will use Growth and go for more training in a job that will help me make more money. Growth will help me in the area of work. I place a blue strip on the stick to help me understand that I will have to deal with sicknesses at times. Truth and Healing are the medicines I need in my life to be healthy. I have my stick tied with red, green, and blue. I have written in my journal, and now I place the* *stick at the wheel outside and let the wind speak to me. (You can place the stick at your personal altar if you do not have a medicine wheel in your life.) I sit in Prayer at the stick and listen and journal ways I can make my life better through the teaching of the stick.*

When finished with the Ceremony, close the bundle and place it back where it goes, to use any time you wish. You can tie new strips onto the stick as often as needed. When you feel the matter that you are working with is completed, you may burn the strip of color or the whole stick. This should be done on the day of the full moon at noon. Remember to cut new strips of the seven colors and replace them in the bundle for the next work you do.

*Note:* Ceremony is the medicine way. You can adjust your Ceremony to fit your needs. Remember to be respectful of all when doing Ceremony. Do not break the laws of the land or harm anyone. You must remember others always when working Ceremony. Ceremony will bring Changes to your life. Never walk in harm's way or with anger in your mind when working Ceremony.

Aho.

# 5 ◆ DARK HEART— THE SNABBERS

I watch the candles glisten in the night. I sit against the wall in the familiar spot, in the North in the teaching lodge. I smell the fresh sage that was placed at the wheel by those who pray tonight. It has been a great evening. I remember the laughter in the room and the tears. I remember their faces glistening. I like to see students learn.

"Gee, Mom, I wish you were here. It's like old days when I was a kid and sat with you. I remember the ones that I sat with, how they listened to your Wisdom. I'm glad you're in the Spirit World where you can guide me. I'm glad I know the truth and I am of the sun, moon, and seven stars. And, more than anything, as I walk into my eldership, I know the way of the Wolf is strong in my heart."

I drop my head and sing a Prayer. I hear the soft, gentle beat of the drum, the call of the glistening path, the sparkling stars. I breathe in and out and start to rise up way beyond my physical mortal life. I stand in the silence of the snow. I hear it touch my hair. I see the large flakes floating. On each flake, there is a light—a tiny star sparkling. I see the glint of color as each snowflake flutters by.

Before me, a bright silver light is vibrating. I walk in the snow, higher into the mountains I go. The voices of the young students echo in my mind, the ones who want to destroy their lives by taking drugs and drinking alcohol, the ones who wish to commit suicide.

"I wonder, Grandfather/Grandmother, why is it that each one of them is not perfect in their own way? Why is it that life scampers away? Is it as the old woman said? Is it only trust? Is it that mankind has broken the circle of trust?"

I hear a cry; a cracking sound, a fierce growling and meowing at the same time. It cuts through the air. I stop. I sense a darkness all around me—it's an eerie feeling. Before me, the road dances and quivers; the sparkling colors, the colors dazzle me. They are vibrant. The road looks as if it is shaking like Jello. It is millions and millions and millions of diamonds.

I don't think about the sound that I heard, and I walk forward. I feel an intense Energy. Songs all around me, drums and flutes, children singing. The Energy grows stronger.

Before me, I see a being, an older man with beautiful long white hair, loose and free. He has a long narrow face, etched with age. Each crevice and wrinkle is sharply defined. His cheekbones are high, his eyes steel blue. He has on a cotton shirt made of orange cloth with small flowers in it. Around his neck, he wears a necklace with seven teeth and four toenails. They are very sharp and pointed. He has on skin pants and boots to his knees that are laced to the top, and from the laces hang more pointed nails; bunches of them cascade down his boot.

He motions with his hand for me to come closer. As I do, I see circles of color, one on his forehead, one in his throat area, one in his chest where his heart is, one in his solar plexus at his abdomen, and one in his reproductive area. Each one of these circles has color.

The one in the reproductive area is red; the one in the stomach area is orange; the one above it in the solarplexus is yellow. Above that the circle in the heart is green; the throat is blue; the forehead is purple; and I can now see he has one on the top of his head that is radiating a beautiful burgundy light.

As I come closer, the colors seem more intense. The circles are perfect vibrating forces the size of a quarter. The colors extends through his body. They light up the area around him. Behind him, I see a camp with a fire glowing softly. I see a bedroll on the ground with bedrolls beside it and a few bundles. A clothesline is tied to the trees, and some rags are hanging over it. On the ground, I see an ax stuck in the side of a tree. Wood is neatly cut and piled.

"I've been waiting on you. Come with me, I have something to say." The spirit turns and walks towards the fire. I follow him. To the right of me, I hear the sound of tree limbs and twigs breaking. I feel movement swiftly cutting through the woods. The ferns move. I hear a low guttural sound, "Arrrrerre, grrreerah."

I walk with the spirit and sit on the log. "Hello, Wolf. I am Tah-no-he, Tah-no-he, Badger Man."

His eyes are small and beady, dark now. I smell a strange odor.

"I am Badger Man," he says again quickly. He reaches and holds onto his necklace.

"Are those the symbol of the badger?" I ask.

"Yes, these are teeth and claws of my great, great ancestors. I represent Energy. I am the totem for Energy. I wish to speak to you of Energy, the power of the smile, the mystery of a secret, the complexity of the yawn. Energy is the fullness and pureness of Power. There is much Energy within the human existence, for all of spirit is Power."

At this moment, from a cliff behind us, a dark shadow jumps into the circle where we sit. I am confronted by a wild bobcat. It sits at the feet of the Badger Man and they look each other in the face. The bobcat has a very soft and sweet look in its eyes. They narrow and close gently. Then the bobcat turns and looks at me. Fear runs all over my body.

"You have no need to be afraid," Badger Man says. "You must know the lesson of limits, and this is the teacher."

In front of my eyes, the bobcat shifts and a lovely young woman emerges with shining chestnut hair and yellow eyes.

"This is Wa-Na-Shoshie. She is Bobcat Woman."

She is stocky and short. Her hair is long and free, her face narrow. She wears a beautiful bobcat skin dress. She just sits beside Badger Man and doesn't speak.

"Bobcat Woman tells me that you are walking in the North, that it is your destiny to teach those who listen about the mind and to give them the understanding of the brain. You are on the sacred path, and I am glad you are here," Badger Man says, a gentleness in his voice.

We sit together, the three of us, and Badger Man and I speak of limits and Energy for a long time.

"It is important that you know the four directions of limits," Badger Man says.

He takes a stick and draws an eye in the ground, the eye of a wolf. He puts a sacred spiral around it in the form of a path. Under the eye, he makes a hole. The path goes around clockwise, until it gets to the top where it goes into spirit. There, on the right side, he draws four holes in the path. On the left side, on the outside of the path, he draws seven stars.

"This is what we call the Wolf's Eye. It is important to know that you walk with the Sacred Sight. Humans see it as the third eye. There is the bear's eye, the wolf's eye, the buffalo's eye, the eagle's eye, the raven's eye, the lynx's eye, and the horse's eye. You walk with the Wolf's eye. These are the Sacred Clans, the Seven Seers, the ones who carry with them the sight of Energy. They can see Balance, Success, and Choice, for they see the Energy, and they see Responsibility. They each know their lessons. The Wolf's is timidity; its direction is North.

The Buffalo's is the lesson of shame, and the direction is above. For the Horse, the lesson is solitude, and the direction is the center. The Eagle's lesson is presumption; its direction is the East. The Bear's lesson is confusion; its direction is West. For the Raven, the lesson is guilt, and its direction is South. For the lynx, the lesson is doubt, and its direction is below.

Enlightenment is the East, innocence is the South, introspection is the West, and Wisdom is the North. Above, below, and within are in the center. It is represented by a crystal rock.

Those are the places where you can go and study with the Spirit Keepers and learn the lesson of limits. Limits is a lesson from the North, Wolf, and it is a lesson that most individuals skip over. I think that it is the Grandfather/Grandmother of all lessons. When you speak of these sacred directions and lessons, it is important to walk to each of those Spirit Keepers and listen to what they teach."

Badger Man smiles. "Lessons are hard to learn in life. They are brought forth from the chemical movement within the physical brain. Our needs are brought forth from chemical reactions. The habits and behavior in the brain are learned patterns brought forth by chemical reaction."

He taps his stick on the ground. "As you teach about the brain, it is important to reflect on the actions of the Spirit Keepers, for they lived first and have great Knowledge. As a humankind, you must find Wisdom and guidance from the Spirit Keepers to understand the thoughts of the mind on your earth walk."

Badger Man points to the sacred drawing. "You must make this. You must gather clay and make an amulet."

He reaches into a pouch he has on his belt and pulls out a red ribbon, a green ribbon, a blue ribbon, and a white ribbon. He holds them out to me and says, "These are the directions—the four directions you walk with. They come from the direction the Wolf comes from. The Wolf is from within. It is the space of the self, for the self is the grandest teacher there is. The four colors are red, standing for excellence; green for expression; blue for abundance; and white for forceful. When you think of "forceful," think of the Power of Grandmother/Grandfather/Great Spirit and the thunder and the lightning, the wind and the fire."

He picks up the colored ribbons. "Tie these in the four holes at the bottom of the clay piece to show that you understand what you walk with. You will want to put your stars on the side of the clay piece, to the left of the spiral. The clay piece will guide you from within. You will have the Power of enlightenment, Wisdom, and the above and below spirit energies. Carry it with you in spirit always."

He holds out the seven colored ribbons and says, "Pick a color."

I choose the green, and he smiles at me. The Bobcat Woman nods her head.

"Doubt is your lesson," Badger Man goes on, "and your direction is Wisdom, which is the North. It is the place of the Wolf and the Buffalo. It is from the Buffalo's Knowledge that you can gain your heart's desire. If the Wolf has doubts, it will drop its head in shame. Do you understand that these are the lessons of the Sacred Colors of Energy, and you are the one who brings the Vision of the seven stars?"

He points to the ground and says, "Draw your Power. Bring forth your amulet."

He draws the hoof of a buffalo on the ground. "For you, Wolf, your Power is Above. In the above world you are a light being. With Buffalo medicine you have the Power of Prayer. You will be able to show your students how to walk with the power of the wolf's eye: this is called the Sweet Medicine of Great Spirit /Creator/ God. It is the Medicine of Energy and Prayer. It is important that when the students learn about Great Spirit/ Creator they know they are using Energy medicine and the Prayer of the Buffalo and the Wolf."

Badger Man smiles at Bobcat Woman.

She shifts to cat and bounds over his shoulder and away into the woods.

"Limits are hard to catch. Limits are hard to keep; limits are hard to set. Limits are control," Badger Man says in a serious tone. "Hand me your bundle."

I hesitate. Is that the right thing to do?

"No, no, hand it to me. Do not sit in doubt. Hand it to me with grace."

I hand it to him with a gentle smile. "You must express yourself in goodness, Wolf. You must let go, you must walk on, you must be the Path. You are moving to a place where you come to the deepest part of humankind—Understanding, which is the voice of the soul. There is the brain/mind and soul; it is the entire North, and the Wolf is the guardian of the North," Badger Man says. "When humankind understands, wholeness is the outcome. Your soul mate holds the Knowledge you seek."

"Seek? I wish I knew where I signed up to seek," I respond.

I feel a spinning. I am dizzy. I drift, my eyes closed. When I open them, I am sitting in a tavern. I look around and I can see out the windows that I must be in a place like New Mexico or Arizona. The bartender sets a glass of water down in front of me and says, "Spirit, girl, you're in Spirit."

"I find it so interesting that the Spirit World and the physical world look so much the same."

"Well, you have to remember that it's all one. What would be the difference in the Creation of Spirit and the creation of Physical Spirit?" He laughs and walks off with a towel over his shoulder.

"Would you like to dance?" I hear a deep, familiar sound. I turn thinking I will see Dark Eyes. It's eerie, for the form is his, but it doesn't have the resonance I am used to.

He reaches out his hand and says, "Try me and see. I am who you know me to be."

He two-steps me and swirls me around the floor, pulling me close to his heart, then pushing me away and spiraling me around. He draws me near, holds me tight and says, "You still think it is not me?"

As we dance around the floor, I become more and more uncomfortable. I push him away.

"I demand that you tell me who you are and what you want. I don't think

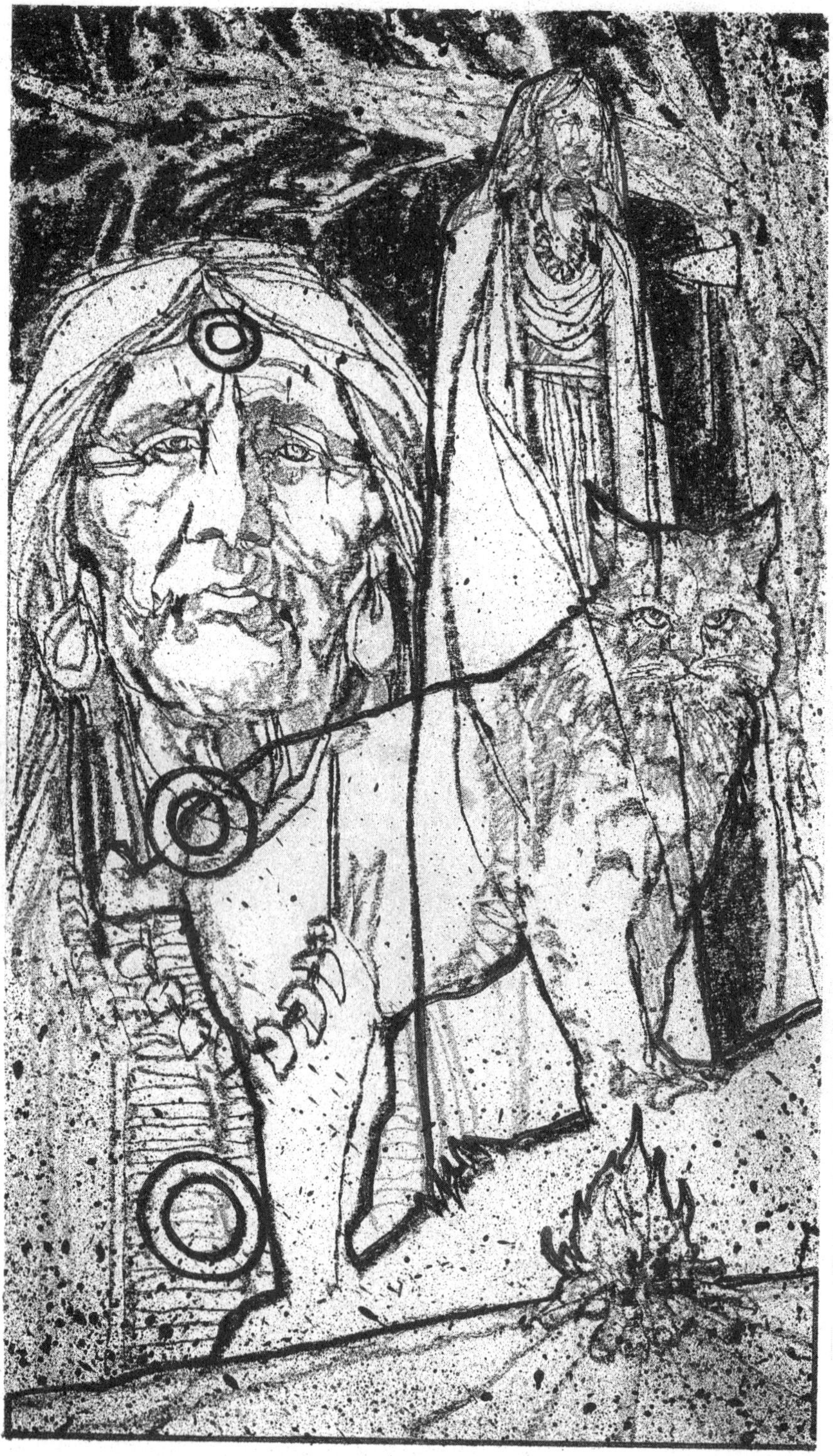

I know you nor do I want to," I say. "Anyone can dance a dance, but I know when it is Dark Eyes and you are not him."

We sit down at the table and the bartender brings two large iced teas.

"See, he knows us," he says. "It is our drink, two iced teas, no lemon, no sugar."

He drinks his tea. His masculine beauty in its elder ship is Dark Eyes, but I know he is not. I know this isn't the man—this isn't the spirit—that I have known for so many years. I know that he let me go, and we have closed that door.

I look at this spirit and say, "We have closed the door, Dark Eyes and I."

"But, you and I," he says, "have not closed the door. Isn't it interesting how a woman is like a desert, and a man's love is the small drops of water that come to quench her thirst?"

I take a deep breath. "I don't hear Dark Eyes. Something is wrong with you if you are him."

He leans back in his chair, crosses his legs, looks at me with a grin in his eyes, and says, "Yeah, isn't life a bitch?"

I look at him and know that he has to be that catty, distant, mischievous spirit I know as King Coyote.

"I created Dark Eyes for you. I control your feelings and emotions, remember," he says. "I know what is ahead for you. The Great Spirit has a plan, but as long as Dark Eyes is your desire, it won't work. You have fallen into the hands of a snabber, Gotcha!!" He lets out a deep laugh.

I feel dizzy and sad. "Are you telling me there is no Dark Eyes, that all there is—is you?" I ask.

"No, Not at all...You see, girl, your heart feeling has brought a love forth and your desires make him real. I just walk around in that pretty mind of yours and conjure up your true love, when really you are acting out of passion and the desire for romance. All humankind are the same," he states, "they let me, their emotions, speak for their mind. They call it their heart speaking. Hearts don't speak or think. I DO!" He laughs.

"Yep, the good OLE South at work. You see you need the voice of emotions, you need fire in your life, and you fall in love with your dreams and passions. My trick, your treat," he says. "I think it's time you know me for who I am. I am Dark Heart, the passion and darkness of all hearts who have been hurt by love—who have been rejected, laughed at, and made to feel inadequate. I want you to learn the lesson of "come-here-go-away," he says.

I look and see only Dark Eyes. At that moment, the bobcat walks in and sits at his feet. I remember that the Bobcat Woman has to do with limits. I look Dark Heart in the eyes, and say, "I think that as humans we give way too much of our energy to affairs of the heart. I think that what I will triumph from is having a solid, clear mind and making the right decision. A young one can fall deep in love in the spring and into bitter hate in the fall. It seems like a lifetime we've gone around this circle, but it's just one life — mine. I have come to the Rainbow Medicine Wheel, to the Vision of the sun, moon, and seven stars to listen to Grandmother and Grandfather Wolf teach me the way of my life. From the time I was a small child up to the time I walked on the earth as a teacher. I am still young. In this wheel, in this setting, I am learning the four directions, I am learning what the spirit, what the body, what the emotions, what the mind — with the brain and the soul — really are. I'm learning enlightenment and innocence are, and what introspection and Wisdom are, and most of all inner peace and Will. It's becoming very clear to me that you must be something inside of me," I say. "You are looking like my thoughts, thoughts that play games."

The strolling guitar players wander up and start to play an upbeat Spanish love song. The sound of the guitars whirls through my mind. I look at Dark Heart's physical beauty, and I know that as soon as the glass of tea is gone, he will be gone, too. And for years this has driven me crazy.

"You are only my thoughts, and I have listened to you and know that we are in Balance," I say. Therefore you are a sweet dream." I grin. "That's right, a sweet dream. And I can wake up any time I choose."

He blows me a kiss from the ends of his fingertips. I feel it graze my cheek. He brushes my hair back and embraces me for another dance. We whirl and turn. I feel his heart against mine, but the darkness of desire is not going to deplete my energy. I let go and drift quietly away in the snow, taking a long night's walk in the moonlight by the river in the ice and the cold.

I see a sweet spirit in front of me — gentle, soft — a baby bobcat. I walk over and sit down by the kitten. I reach for it, but it hisses and scratches me. Then it bites me. What pain! I begin to cry. Am I crying because of the bite or the pain from Dark Eyes? Emotions are very hard to live with and are not supposed to follow you to the spirit world, I think.

"I bit you with passion," I hear.

The kitten is now Dark Heart — a strong male spirit. He looks a lot like Dark Eyes.

"What's the problem? Didn't you know there are more the one of me?" he asks. "You are in the lesson of limits. Make your Choice. Will you set your limits or suffer?"

"I just really want to understand," I say. "I think the hardest thing to understand as a humankind is that the South has many emotions. So I guess you have come to teach me something, right? Who did you say you are?"

"I told you—I am passion, your passion," Dark Heart says. "All humankind has illogical emotions. They test you and give life spice. It's not so bad, really. It makes life interesting," he smiles. "When it comes to the thoughts of humankind, I can be a dream or a nightmare. Yes, I have come so that you can Understand that it's okay to have a soul mate, but you will need passion and romance—the love of your life. I, Dark Heart, bid for your hand. It is I—the strongest spirit of all—who will sweep you away and make you mine."

"LEAVE," I hear a voice say.

Badger Man is standing face to face with him.

"You have no control here. You are her emotions, and you know it. There will be no trickery here. She can make her own Choices. She will show her Colors, and you be gone now," Badger Man says. "Set your limits, girl! Show him your boundaries."

"Okay," I say. "I understand passion and romance and I want to meet my soul mate. It is always a push and pull with both of you. Maybe the Balance comes with the Blue-Eyed Raven. I was taught you must beware of passion because it can get you in trouble." I say.

Badger Man sits on a rock.

"Listen, Dark Heart," he says, "you are passion and romance—illogical emotions—you are forbidden and will cause heartache. She seeks the Knowledge of the North, which is wholeness, and she will find it in knowing her soul mate. It's time for you to tell her the truth.

"You are the emotions and thoughts," Badger Man goes on. "She is the brain/mind. You are the feelings and emotions. You are the South and she is the North. You like to dance with her, but she has come to learn that there are four parts to the humankind—emotions, brain, mind, and soul" says Badger Man.

"I think there is a part of the story that comes to light in the North and that is the soul. She will feel soul Energy with the Blue-Eyed Raven. The North and South are the Blue Road and all humankind seeks wholeness. The truth of life is that the Brain is a ball of Energy and the Balance of that Energy happens when the Blue Road is understood." Badger Man smiles. "What brings humankind into Balance is to listen to the mind, the voice of the spirit and have a strong soul connection."

"I think you should ask her who she picks and why. I think I am more then just a Choice." Dark Heart says.

"I think I can answer that," I say. "You say you are passion, right? And Dark Eyes is romance, right?"

"You got it, little lady. Passion, at your service," he smiles and his eyes glisten.

"I see," I reply.

"Well, feelings are many, and when one goes another appears. If you don't want Dark Eyes, then you have me," Dark Heart says.

"All she has to do is know the emotions and the need for the soul and all is in Balance," Badger Man says.

"Let me tell you about your soul mate, the Blue-Eyed Raven. He is Balance and Truth for you. You know that, Dark Heart. Each person must be careful to listen to the mind and the needs of the soul. If emotions and negative thoughts run rampant, the soul is affected. They cause black holes in the soul. Those are the dark spots of life.

"Remember the Snabbers, illogical emotions like to cause pain. They are the illnesses of the brain; they imbalance our thoughts. They are temptation. They bring challenge and fantasy, passion and romance, darkness and pain. The Snabbers are the evildoers—and they are all parts of King Coyote. He invents your desires and passions to control you. Snabbers feed on the soul of all humankind. When they do their feeding, your soul looks like Swiss cheese—all hole-y." He grins.

" Wolf, you have been brought here to understand that you and the South are on the Blue Road. It is time to see and understand marriage. The Blue-Eyed Raven will be with you soon. You must understand that you are carrying the lizard bag—it is the Will of Great Spirit."

"Before there were humankind there was the soul. The soul is the spiritual pathway that brings forth your spirit. The soul is Great Spirit Energy. It is the Power of good. The soul is the path we all must travel to live as humankind and remember life in the beginning, which is known as 'the Mystery.'

"The spirit is words and words are Color. Color is medicine that brings force and life. The stars hold the story Mystery and the Wolf sings the song," Badger man says softly

"Yes, that is all well and good, and this Blue-Eyed Raven sounds like a great deal, but what about love and romance and FUN? Sounds like all he is going to do is bore her to death," Dark Heart says.

He turns to me." I think you really need to listen to your thoughts. Are you sure you want to be like all the other humankind?"

He reaches in his pocket and pulls out a clear crystal stone. He looks at it and thinks for a moment. Then he says, "Marriage and kids and blah,

blah, blah. Want to talk about limits—there are limits! You'll give up and settle like all the rest of humankind. A little house and kids!"

I turn away from them and there is the river before me. I love winter at the river—it is calm, quiet, and peaceful. There is ice along the shore and ice in the trees as the sun comes up. The ice sings and sparkles. I think of him, his deep voice and gentle dark eyes. How can there be another? I want to stay here with him. I don't need to have a soul connection—to understand my soul. Dark Eyes is my soul. I love passion and romance. It can't be over. He can't be gone. The Wolf is to be wild...

**I hear the howl of the wolf calling me back.**

## THE TEACHINGS OF ENERGY— BADGER MEDICINE

We are all Energy, nothing we do or have is not Energy. As we live our lives, we need to look at the way we apply our Energy. Are we using it as a medicine to treat Life's lessons, or are we wasting Energy by not having limits and good teachings?

To have a healthy mind, the Energies of the brain must be Balanced. This happens when we live a life with limits and good thoughts. Take care of the physical brain chemistry—it's self. Live a life with spiritual teachings that guide us to live our Vision and achieve our dreams. Live a life of goals and low stress. To live with low stress, you need to apply your Energies in a positive, creative way.

Energy is spirit and supplies the breath of Life. It is important to know what you want out of Life. It is important to learn to listen to your teachers and to know what to do in matters of illness and stress.

To gain the highest levels of Energy, it is essential to take care of your physical brain, by having plenty of rest and eating and drinking right. That means no alcohol, no drug use. Allow yourself to listen to the mind, which will feed your spirit. Daily prayer, long walks, studying spirituality, and shamanic journeying can help you arrive at those high levels of Energy.

The totem of Energy is the Badger, symbolizing high Energy and aggressive action. It is achievement—never giving in or giving up.

Aho.

## THE LESSON OF LIMITS

A limit is drawing the line.

> **Example:** *You will not lie to yourself or others; you will not drink or use drugs. You will not do anything to harm others, like gossiping, hitting others, or owning a weapon that can cause death.*

As we walk on the Earth Mother, we are living with lessons. When we get tired of lessons and feel we can't take another one, we are in the Balance of limits, for we have to say we have had enough. This is a boundary and that is a Limit.

Limits may be as easy as having your day outlined and following the schedule. The problem with limits is stress: the stress of not having your way, not understanding laws and rules, having to take care of yourself, worrying and not having control. As you learn this lesson you'll see that there are reasons for boundaries and limits.

Limits save our lives and keep us safe. We as humankind need to set boundaries and have limits in our life. It is the way to stop abuse.

> **Example:** *If people are out of order, angry, and hurtful, you will ask them to settle down or leave the place in which they are acting up. Until you learn the lesson of limits, you can use up a lot of Energy trying to fit in, trying to be liked by others, or trying to hold onto a job.*

Limits are a lesson in the brain and mind, because they bring forth the safety that reduces the stress of worry, of taking actions in your life that have no goals, of fear-related actions, of doing things you don't want to do, but can't say no—of doing anything that is abusive to your self.

You can make your Choices and live your life as you wish when you know the lesson of limits.

Aho.

# THE WOLF'S EYE AMULET

An amulet is a medicine piece, usually a bag or a necklace made especially to protect you. It holds magical powers that you place in it with a special color or bead. It is a lucky and powerful object. You can make it from clay or rock or whittle it from wood. It balances your thoughts and brings safety to your life.

**Tools:** *You'll need Mexican clay, or any pottery clay, or sculpture clay (if you use sculpting clay, you'll end up with a red clay color and you'll need to bake it and then paint it). You can use a product called Sculpy, which is a molding color substance used for sculpting (I like to use it, because it doesn't bleed and you can get it in a natural red color or in other colors, if you wish, and it doesn't bleed. You don't have to paint it.); a sculpting knife; paper towels to clean your hands; sculptinghardener, or fingernail polish, or you can coat the Wolf's Eye with a thin coat of glue. This way, your piece will be strong and will not bleed should it get wet (Clay, Mexican Clay, and potting clay all have a tendency to bleed.)*

The Wolf's Eye is a flat piece that can be three to five inches (7.5 to 12.5cm) in diameter. Roll out your clay so that you have a long piece that you can make into a spiral by rolling it on the outer edges of itself. You'll want to flatten the spiral anywhere from about one-quarter of an inch to a half inch (6 to 12mm) thick, depending upon on how thick you want your amulet.

After you have made the spiral, smooth off the inside circle with your sculpting knife, so that you can draw a wolf's eye. After you have drawn the eye, move down to the right-hand corner and make four holes in the piece so you can tie on your four direction ribbons. Also, make a hole underneath the eye. You can do this by taking a large nail and pressing it through the clay. On the upper right-hand side of the medallion, place your spiral totem. This will be a drawing of a hoofprint of one of the seven animal guides.

On the left-hand side of the amulet, draw the seven stars. These represent the seven Spirit Keepers, the seven Colors, the seven medicines, and the seven Lessons of the Wolf's Eye Amulet.

Next, you'll need to cut pieces of ribbon to tie into your directions to represent the words:

**Red:** Excellence;
**Green:** Expression;
**Blue:** Abundance;
**White:** Forceful.

These are the words that it takes to handle your life adequately, to keep you Balanced. You'll also need to choose a ribbon of your favorite color; this is your "within" color that you tie in the center of the medallion. Slide your ribbon through the hole, and then tie a large knot in the back. This will hold the ribbon in place.

Each Spirit Keeper has a color, medicine word and a lesson connected with it. You can follow the chart and apply the power of the chart teachings:

| Color | Animal | Medicine Word | Lesson Word |
| --- | --- | --- | --- |
| Red | Eagle | Enlightenment | Presumption |
| Orange | Raven | Innocence | Guilt |
| Yellow | Buffalo | Above | Doubt |
| Green | Horse | Below | Solitude |
| Blue | Bear | Introspection | Confusion |
| Purple | Lynx | Wisdom | Ignorance |
| Burgundy | Wolf | Within | Timidity |

You can change the color of the ribbon you tie in the center to what ever color is right for the animal you are working with. To achieve the hoofprint or the paw print of the animal you are working with, the vision follows.

## VISION OF THE TOTEM ANIMAL FOOT OR HOOFPRINT

Find a place where you will not be disturbed and sit quietly. Get very comfortable. Breathe in through your nose and out through your mouth gently and relax. Let go of all your thoughts and envision a pathway before you, one that you feel comfortable walking upon. As you walk, you'll see animals—the wolf, the buffalo, the horse, the lynx, the eagle, the raven, and the bear. They will appear to you at various times.

When you have seen one particular animal four separate times, come back from your vision work and record the animal in your journal. This animal will be your working totem connected to the Wolf's Eye Amulet.

When you have connected with the animal, tie its color ribbon to your amulet and know that it is your guide, comforter, and protector in the spirit world. The animal you select can change. If you should see one of the seven animals four times in a dream, that is a message is to change the color and work with the new animal. Your totem animal will allow you to place its paw print or hoofprint on your amulet. It will be your guardian until such time as you have a new animal and change the hoofprint or the paw print.

Keep the amulet with you at all times. You can put it in a pouch, wear it, or place it beside you on a table. It is there to help you understand how to balance your energy. The following questions will also help:

**1. List your balance of energy.** How do you eat? How do you sleep? How do you spend your time? How do you waste your time? What causes confusion? What upsets you? What do you get angry at most often?

It is a good idea to journal this each day, and try to put it into Balance by Understanding that a proper diet, proper rest, not wasting time or being confused and upset, will help you build and strengthen your Energy.

**2. List your limits.**
    a. How far are you willing to go in destroying yourself? It is important to answer with your true negative behaviors. Then, for a change to take place, ask yourself if these Energies are what you would like to live with forever.

**3. Choose a direction color.** This will show the action you want to use to Balance your energy daily, weekly, or monthly. Choose from one of the four colors and apply the word to your life on a daily basis. For example:

*Red*: Excellence. Each day of your life, understand that you are living as excellently as you can today. If you do not feel that you are expressing excellence, make a list of the ways you can obtain a better lifestyle. Seek out people who can help you, opportunities that open doors for you, and walk on that color (live your life that way).

*Green*: Expression. Apply yourself. Don't close down, lock up, and listen to old tapes in your mind (by old tapes, I mean things that have been told to you that have caused you to be quiet and not express yourself). Voice your thoughts in an open, solid, and forceful way, for this is how you can expand your Energy and bring words out of your mouth.

*Blue*: Abundance. Living an abundant life comes from understanding what you need and the difference between your needs and wants. Wants sometimes (most times) are trivial and frivolous—spending too much money, living for other people, and wanting to be like other people—whereas needs are your pathway. Every human has needs; diet, rest, relaxation, Understanding, education, interaction, and compassion. Live with abundance. Don't stifle yourself and feel that you are loved by any spirit for being weak, meek, or inadequate.

*White*: Forceful. Lots of people misunderstand and think that "force" is bad. Living forcefully means that you have drive, you have exuberance, you have zest, you have wherewithal, and in this case, forceful means stepping out with the faith that your Creator holds you in its palm and guides you in a safe walk on the Earth Mother.

Follow the Color definitions in the back of the book. And remember, white is the Color of spirit. Apply spirit and all will go in a good way.

**4. List your fears, your angers, your doubts, and the things that you hate.** When you have listed these things, recognize that they are what evil is—what bad is. They are what wrong is, for from these actions you deplete your energy. Do not give time to people who weaken you, to thoughts that break you down, to temptations that overcome you. Look at your list daily, and very carefully. Keep up with the things that bother you and understand that, by holding your Wolf's Eye amulet, you can find guidance through the four

Directions. You can understand that you are an excellent person with the power of self-expression, living an abundant life of forceful Will. You can draw from the Power of the path of Rainbow Medicine, the home of the Energy that feeds Wolf Medicine. You can understand that you do not have to succumb to things that you do not want to do. Don't settle for second best or for passion or romance. Do not settle for the emptiness of the human two-legged life, but listen to the Directions. Look within the Wolf's Eye and walk past the things that weaken you. When you look in your journal, you will see where your Energy is leaking out. You can find what is keeping you from knowing what is yours, what is keeping you living in excuses and blame. You will see that it is you yourself who darkens your heart and closes your mind. You will see that it is you who can make the choice to open your life to a stronger and better way.

Aho.

# 6 ◆ THE BLUE-EYED RAVEN—PRAYER

---

I breathe in and out gently seven times. I find myself walking along the beach. It is cold and ice laces the shore. Behind me, everything inland is frosted and deep in snow. In front of me is the perpetual motion of the ocean as waves crash and roll in. I blow my breath and feel the cold.

Before me I see a hut built of driftwood with smoke coming from the chimney. I recognize this as the house of an old friend of mine. It will be good to see her. I come close to the hut and I remember her gentle voice speaking of the queen and king—the queen of hearts and the king of diamonds. I remember the tarot warnings of the dark-eyed one who could sweep my heart away. Maybe he isn't Dark Eyes, but Dark Heart. It will be good to speak to Gray Wolf and find out.

She is an old seer, one who walks on the Earth plane, and is ridiculed and called crazy. She was locked away in her childhood and studied by experts in psychology. I remember her telling me how interesting it is that no one really wants to know you until they think you know something.

Standing close to the hut, I feel her presence. I turn and see her. Her one blue eye catches me. Her long scraggly hair is white, and her face is wrinkled with stories. "It's good to see you, sister."

"And you, Wolf," she smiles. She walks with a cane. Time has passed, and she is no longer as chipper and spry as I remember, but I can see the distance in the blue eye. I know that she has looked beyond the mysteries of the sea and she has words for me.

"Come in and warm yourself. What a beautiful jacket, all wolf hair." She opens the door and we go inside. "I see you have come to ask one more time which direction to take."

I look around the hut and each piece of wood is aged with the story of the ocean. There are sharks' teeth, whales' teeth; tusks of the walrus; seagull and osprey feathers; all types of sand dollars; sand urchins and sea urchins, and other sea creatures that she has found and dried and made into necklaces and hung in groupings around the room.

"Sit, Wolf," she says, as she points to a cup of tea. "I promise, it's your favorite peach tea."

"Yeah, right," I laugh. "Knowing you, you've got something in it."

"No, no, I don't," she says.

I take a deep breath and let it out. "It seems as if my Grandmother/Grandfather Wolf have someone in store for me."

"Ah, yes," she nods. "It is the Blue-Eyed Raven, the one who waits, the one who comes to you and guides you, the best friend of the wolf—the raven. But in your case soul mates."

"Hmm," I say. "What a strange term, soul mates."

I can see she has something she is thinking about. She has a look she gets when she is about to step into a teaching from spirit.

"No, not at all," she says. "You see, the soul is a path and the path looks like one single road, when really it is one side for going up and one for coming down. Soul mates are the male and female in human form. The female—you—one side of the path and the male—the Blue-Eyed Raven—the other. It takes two sides in the physical reality to make one soul."

"What about Dark Eyes?" I ask.

"Well, that's easy to answer," she replies. "In the spirit we are one—no male or female. In spirit we are part of the Blue Road, the physical road. As all creations, we are part Blue Road and part Red Road. The Blue Road is the physical and the Red Road is the spiritual. All humankind needs to know that it has all emotions and thoughts. They need to realize that to have a healthy soul, they have to balance their emotions, and that means walking with King Coyote.

"Yes, that one is easy. It is where the lessons are learned. In spirit we have no ways except Truth and Balance. I told you that you are the Queen of Hearts, and that is so. You are the one of love and Balance—the path, the soul. It is time for your half-side to come to you. Then you will be whole and the lessons from Dark Eyes will have reason, "she states.

"You are the Wolf, the White Wolf Woman, the North. There is a medicine from the North—it is Prayer, dolphin medicine, and the lesson of expectations that you're having such trouble with," she says.

"Expectations, Wolf," she grins. "Sometimes we need to pray and remember. When we are in Prayer we are walking the soul path. You are going to receive a gift from Great Spirit—your half-side. You come in Prayer to receive the Strength of your best friend, your soul mate." She nods.

" Expectations are your relationship with Dark Eyes. We get in trouble on the Earth Mother when we lose touch with Prayer and get involved in expectations. Am I clear?" she asks.

"I think I'm beginning to understand," I say.

" You and all humankind must learn the lesson of expectations. You need to watch out for their negative energies. When we are in the spirit world and live as spirits, we are Energy, pure Color. Our thoughts give form, and form brings about matter. We all expect our lives go as we wish or want them to. There is a need for Understanding of this lesson, " she says.

"When you have expectations, you can be fooling yourself." She points to the wall where there is a big stick with a fork in the top of it. "Your soul mate is the straight part of the stick; the top, the fork, is expectations, You think Dark Eyes is the love of your life, but really that is only in your thoughts. He has taught you as you teach others. It is time for the straight part of the stick, your soul mate—the Blue-Eyed Raven. The wonder of it all is that you, Dark Eyes, and the Raven are all Great Spirit's Will." She laughs.

I smile. "Yes," I say. "It is so good to be in your presence again."

"And you, Wolf. I'm glad you stopped by my hut. I'm glad you came in the coldness of the winter. It is a lot like expectations, the lesson of the Seals. You know, living at the ocean is the book of Knowledge, filled with the stories of those that saw, and the little ones that hide underneath the ferns—the ones who scurry under the rocks at sunset. It is the place of mysteries that sing the song of the dolphin. Listen."

She opens the door and I hear the sounds of the dolphins. They are jumping this way and that.

"They have told me something that you will want to hear, Wolf. They have told me about the pastel rainbow that arcs from the ocean, the one you must follow that takes you to the face. You face the lines, you walk with the Knowledge of who, what, when, where, why, which, that, this, then."

Gray Wolf and I stand in the door of the hut and watch the moonlight dance on the dolphins. It glistens and sparkles. Interweaving circles of color rise in the sky, making a sacred spiral of color.

"There, Wolf, the soft pastels of spirit are calling. Not long from now, you will stand in the circle, in the center of spirit. Centerology, this is the coming together of all humankind. It is when each human comes to an Understanding of all, when our thoughts are one drumbeat." She pats me on the shoulder. "Remember old Grandmother Four Crows—she taught us we all are one thought. A thought has no beginning and no end."

My mind drifts; I feel myself relax.

"Roll out that bundle," she says. "I've kept it here for you."

She points to the corner, and there is a sleeping bundle. I unroll it, and in the center is a burgundy blanket, thick and padded. I stretch it out in front of the fire. I put my hands behind my head and the songs of the dolphin fill my mind.

I hear the door open, and a small one enters carrying a prayer bundle. She greets me with a nod. I have not seen her on the trail for a long time.

She goes to the other side of the large fireplace and sits down. She lays out in front of her a prayer cloth, some tobacco, and colored cloths.

"What have you come here for, Small One?"

She looks at me with love in her eyes. "I come to pray for soul mates. I've come here to Gray Wolf's by the ocean because the Stairway of Love is showing itself tonight. I do nothing anymore but pray for soul mates, Wolf. It's my job. I spend my time with young ones, teaching them how to be married, showing them the power of their marriage pot."

I breathe in and out with the pace and the rhythm of the waves that crash into the shore. Then I take a deep breath and let it out. I stand, looking my expectations in the face.

There in front of me is the tall one. He is handsome. His eyes are blue. He is soft and gentle, though large in stature. His hair is thinning; his head is round and full. He has a beautiful beard, brownish red, and a potbelly. He is cloaked in a full length black coat. I can see his boots, black in color. His jeans and shirt are black too. He is wearing a necklace that is made of seven amethyst crystals. It hangs over his heart. He holds his black hat in his hand, and on the side of his hat are long raven feathers.

"I've been waiting for you, Wolf. I am the Blue-Eyed Raven. We have spoken and we have interacted, but it is our time now. Come with me."

He turns and walks away. I follow him up a path — higher we go, longer we travel. We reach the top and he sits, and I sit, and the sun sets. The colors are beautiful, bright oranges and deep rich purples, and burgundy. He holds a beautiful pot in his hand. It is made of clay, very simple and round. He hands it to me.

"Half of the pot is yours and half of the pot is mine. Together we will bring it forth and draw from its powers. We will always have food and water, and we will always walk together as the raven and wolf on the Earth Mother."

He shakes the pot, tips it over, and a ring tumbles out into his hand. It is a beautiful ruby, rich and burgundy, surrounded by seven sea pearls, set on a beautiful, pink gold band. The ruby is shaped like a four-cornered diamond.

"Hold out your hand, if you would be my lady."

I extend my hand and he places the ring on my finger. "I am not binding you, I am not owning you, I am asking you to fly with me," he says with a sweet grin.

"I cannot fly, but I can run," I say.

"Will you?"

"As long as you let me be free, as long as you know that I am a wolf, not a raven," I reply. "I have learned the lesson of expectations. I know a seal is not a dolphin. We are very similar to them, the wolf and raven, the seal and the dolphin. Have you seen the spiraling rainbow path that takes you higher into spirit?" I ask him.

"Yes, I have. Bring the pot and come with me." He takes off and moves through the woods with the flight of a raven. I follow with the Power of the wolf. We reach a pathway that is sacred and shimmering in pale color. He soars ahead and I follow.

"Through the years on Earth, we have been husband and wife forever. We have brought forth life in the laughter of children. We watch them peek out from behind the trees and call from the parks and enter from the streets. We help them grasp the disappointments of expectations."

"Your marriage is the legacy of soul mates," I hear an old one's voice say. "You, Wolf, take you, Blue-Eyed Raven—you, Blue-Eyed Raven, take you, Wolf. . . The Rainbow Medicine Wheel has brought wholeness to your life, Wolf. The Blue-Eyed Raven is your half-side, your soul mate. You are complete now," the old one says."

"The queen and king, yes," Gray Wolf says.

"Two best friends become one heart on earth and in spirit. You are home in each others' mind," says the old one.

"Wait—what about Dark Eyes?" I ask.

He appears.

"I am you and you are me—the North and the South. We are the emotions and thoughts, the brain and the mind. When you walk on the earth you have a half-side, the Blue-Eyed Raven. It is a good thing, I guess. As all Humankind, you need to marry and he is your soul mate. I am your heart," he smiles.

"You are the path—the way of healing. You and I are the thoughts of the mind. You will complete your dance with your soul mate. It is very important that you and the Blue-Eyed Raven are one. He is your soul's voice and will guide you on earth as you walk your vision. It is like black and white—you are the white and he is the black—together you walk as balance. Many will see your commitment and love and this will give others inner peace." Dark Eyes says.

"I'm always here " he points to his heart.

"What the medicine wheel is teaching you is to listen to the voice of your spirit—that is heart talk from the mind, I am that heart talk for you," he says.

"Never worry, for we are together always. Never worry for we are together always. We are the love. With no love there is no magic. Nothing can ever break the bond of love. It is the metaphysical conduit that allows the Energy of Great Spirit to flow between two spirits. You are the mind and I am the heart..."

The Blue-Eyed Raven and I make our dance around the circle. We go from north to east, and east to south, from south to west, and west to north. We pass the babies, the young ones, the adults; we dance past the elders, and they smile.

"You stand in Prayer now," the old voice says, and I look into Grandfather Wolf's eyes. Joy fills my heart as I see him. I turn and

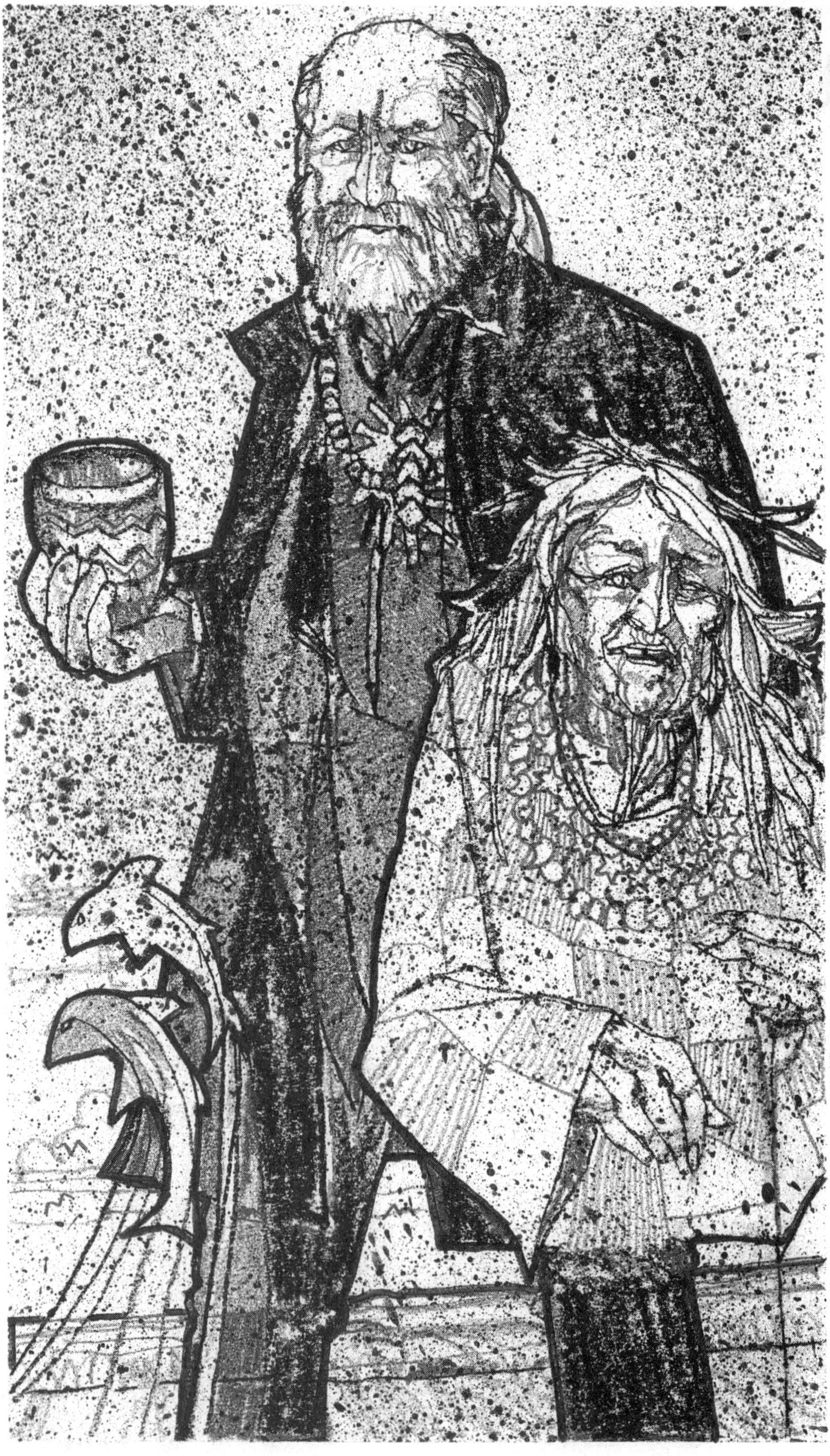

Grandmother Wolf is there behind us. They are standing in the West and the East. In the North and South stand the twins, the wolf and the coyote. They hold two blankets, a blue one from North to South, and a red one from East to West. Raven stands toward the Southwest and I stand toward the Northeast. They wrap us with the blankets.

"You are now entwined forever in your hearts and in your walk." The Small One offers a prayer. "I hold this marriage pot full of love and compassion that each have walked their lessons."

I feel the soft gentle kiss he gives me in the sunshine. I pledge my love eternally and I know the depth of Prayer that I have petitioned for all my life. I whisper in his ear that I hope all humankind find this love. I see Grandfather/Grandmother Wolf's hands—the dark paw and the light paw. I see the couples around the circle show their Strength in love as they all hold hands, completing the circle.

I awaken walking in the snow.

"Fear not, Granddaughter," I hear the soft voice of Grandmother Wolf. "No dream has touched your mind. Your mind has brought reality to your physical brain, for on the earth plane, you walk with the Raven. Here in spirit, you are joined by the love of the path, by the magic of the marriage pot. Marriage brings forth birth and you must birth the story, walk the other stones, and open the doors, for you face the Vision of Great Spirit. You carry the legacy of Truth, and the song of the coyote and wolf brings harmony. When that occurs, inner peace is at hand. Follow the stones to Will, make a right turn to Sweet Medicine, and take the walk of the Impeccable Journey. It lies ahead of you, Granddaughter."

The wind circles my ears and sweetly kisses me on the nose.

**I hear the howl of the wolf calling me back.**

# THE TEACHINGS OF PRAYER— DOLPHIN MEDICINE

Prayer is the act of communication between your mind (spirit) and the spirit world. Prayer is pure spiritual Energy. The Energy brings forth Power and enlightenment from Great Spirit. Prayer is an action that Balances and clears the mind.

When you are in Prayer, you use spiritual language. You are able to focus on your needs and desires. You open your mind in such a way that you can make Changes throughout your total existence. The spirit totem for prayer is the Dolphin, for it is the symbol of flow and fluid motion.

Prayer works miracles: it heals the sick, comforts the old and those in grief. It is the voice of your Vision and dreams. Healing takes place as you pray, for there is peace and Tranquility, warmth, and love in Prayer. Prayer is for all people; all are welcomed by Grandfather/Grandmother/Great Spirit/Creator/God.

In the teachings of Rainbow Medicine we bring forth Prayers in the form of a prayer tie. This is a Native American way of praying. To make Prayer ties, you use tobacco, a symbol for the Earth Mother, cloth, and a symbol of living things such as plants and trees. You can use paper napkins to save cloth and get the colors you want, since paper napkins come in many true colors.

## PRAYER TIES

**Tools:** *Loose tobacco; cloth or paper napkins in the colors red, orange, yellow, green, blue, purple, burgundy, cut into one-inch (2.5cm) squares; string; a stick 12" (30cm) long; smudge supplies.*

Use a cloth or paper napkin that is the Color of the medicine you are praying with.

> **Example:** *If you want to pray for Color in your life. Use red cloth or paper. If you want to pray for Energy, use orange; for Prayer, use yellow; for Courage, use green; for Understanding, blue; for Knowledge, purple; for Will, use burgundy.*

Place a pinch of tobacco in the center of the square. Make a wad or little bundle by gathering up the corners of the cloth and tying the string around the top of the bundle.

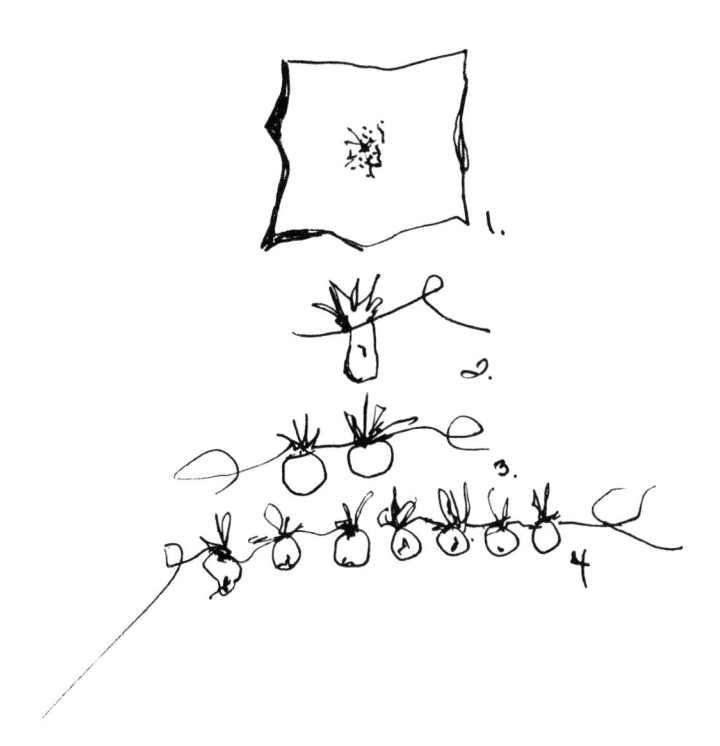

Move on to make another Prayer bundle and tie it on the line. Tie as many bundles as you need—one or several for each prayer you have. When you are done with your prayer ties, tie them to the stick and place them on your altar or at the Medicine Wheel to be burned on the day of the full moon. As the prayers are released in the fire, the smoke carries them to Great Spirit. You can also hang the Prayers as you tie them, in the trees or on a fence in your yard, and let the elements do away with them. When the prayers hang outside, it is said that the spirit deer comes and carries the prayers to the spirit world. Then, on the solstice, take what is left of the prayer lines and burn them.

Do your prayer ties daily.

Aho!

# MARRIAGE POT

**Tools:** *A clay pot (a water pot) made by yourself or by another; paint; glue; pieces of cloth; beads; doodads; small souvenirs; keys; matchbook covers; buttons; all types of goodies that you've saved, maybe your Boy Scout or Girl*

*Scout pin (Gather them together between the two of you.); your journal and pen; smudging supplies; a special candle of a color chosen by the couple.*

Note: If you buy the pot, look at the price and see what the total is.

**Example:** *86 dollars and 50 cents. Add the numbers together: 8+6+5+0=19 is 1+9=10, is 1+0=1. This total will indicate the color of the pot: 1 red, 2 orange, 3 yellow, 4 green, 5 blue, 6 purple, and 7 burgundy, 8 red, 9 orange.*

This will also dictate the reading number for the medicine of the pot and the lessons you will be tested with.

**Example:** *1 — Red; Medicine word, Color; Lesson: Trust.*

Make the lesson your goal and treat your life with the medicine. Color in this case, is 1, so treat your life with Color. If you make the pot, I cannot tell you how to decide this; it is up to you.

When you have a finished pot, sit with it together, you and your soul mate (the one you are going to marry). Frequently, we marry a stranger, and then have to go our own way and find our soul mate. It's important that we marry our soul mate. Soul mates are easy to recognize, for they look like yourself.

The two of you smudge, perform the Sacred Herb Ceremony, cleanse your aura, center yourselves, and Balance your thoughts. The marriage pot will hold the value of your sacred union. You will be gluing and painting and attaching all of your special items to the pot that make the two of you one. From this pot will come the birth of your children. For as you put your objects together, the two of you will come together in your likes and dislikes. Then you will reach out into the world and find the essence of your children.

Take a day to sit with your pot before you do your union Ceremony. If you're already married, you can do this Ceremony on your anniversary. Gather all your goodies—these objects are known as medicine objects. They tell the story of your life. You might want to add more to the pot—a painting or a drawing or even a pathway of small stones—if you don't have enough goodies to cover the whole medicine pot.

The pot represents your purpose. The hollowness of the pot is the voice of the wind where Grandfather/ Grandmother/Great Spirit brings forth the life of your marriage. If you've been married a long time and have children and grandchildren, you simply bring forth the symbol of your marriage, of your unity, and your children. It is a wonderful bonding Ceremony to celebrate with your family.

Before you bring your pot forth and complete it, write the following questions in one of your journals, and then talk about them and answer them in your journals. Often these questions will help you figure out where what you call your "wrongs" happened. In other words, where did you go off the track?

1. Who are we together?
2. What is our purpose?
3. What are our beliefs?
4. What will we do every day when we are united?

   **Example:** *who will do the cooking? Who will do the cleaning? Who will take care of the children? Who will do the bulk of the work? Who will do the bookkeeping?*

5. Will we have children?
   a. When?
   b. Why?
   c. How will we teach them?
   d. Where do we want them to go when they are grown?
   e. What will be their beliefs?
   f. What will they give back to the Earth for their existence?
   g. What are their names? (One for each gender Choice.) If you already have a family, look back and recall what you thought when you first married; then also write how you influenced your children to

become what they are. If you did not influence them, who did? Why did you not influence them? Also, list their names and what you wanted to name them, and why you gave them their names.
6. What is our belief about death?
7. What will be our work? Our professions?
8. What education will we have?
9. Where do we want to live?
10. What is our favorite climate?
11. What do we believe about money?
12. What is our belief about our mental health?
13. What will we do when we have grandchildren and great grandchildren? What do we want to do for them?
14. Which name do we use as our last name? If you've chosen the male's name, have you as a male spoken to her about why you have given her your name, and why it is the name you bring forth? Or, are you just doing what the world says you should do? If you choose to use her name, why are you using her name? In other words, what is the purpose of your last name?

## THE LESSON OF EXPECTATIONS—
## SEAL MEDICINE

When you are learning the lesson of expectations you are learning about an action that brings a lot of stress to your life. Expectations open you to thoughts of fantasy and the lower world. In the daily life of a humankind it is important to live—not with Expectations—but with the direction of your Vision or the teachings of your family.

When you assume, conjure, manipulate, or think your life will go in a particular way you want it to, you are acting with expectations. The lesson to be learned is that you are the Energy of Great Spirit. You have the ability to do many things in life, but you are a part of more than just yourself. Learning the lesson of expectations means accepting others and all forms of life on the Earth Mother. You are a part of the web of life—not set apart with the ability to choose your destiny or control your life, and not unlike anyone else.

You will need to apply the medicine of Prayer to calm your expectations. The effect of Prayer will be to bring Balance to your expectations by allowing you to focus and hear messages from your spiritual knowing.

Expectations open your life to pain and hurt. As you try to control your life, a lot of disappointments will come your way, because you cannot bring your own destiny into form. Expectations are not reality-based thoughts; they are illogical, involving you in exaggeration, worry, and stress, and emotions such as fear and anger, and illusions of passion and romance.

Aho!

### EXERCISE IN THE LESSON OF EXPECTATIONS

Take your journal and pen and work with the lesson of expectations. Answer the following questions in your journal.

1. What do you expect out of life?
2. Who do you expect the most from in your life?
3. What do you expect you are entitled to in life?
4. How do you expect the weather to be daily?
5. What do you expect and demand of yourself?
6. What do you expect from Grandfather/Grandmother/Great Spirit/Creator/God?
7. What do you expect from a marriage or friendship or relationship?
8. What do you expect from your children, grandchildren, or great grandchildren?

When you have answered these questions, go over them again and make sure that you have answered them thoroughly and honestly. Then understand the answer that goes along with expectations.

**Answer:** What you expect out of anything is an expectation and will create anxiety.

It is important to understand that the only thing you can do in life is accept what comes. Accept that as humans we have great expectations, and sometimes they are overpowering, overwhelming, and overbearing. Understand that the lesson of expectations is much like the plight of the seal. A man goes out to fish and wants the fish for himself, but the seal beats him to it. So he picks up a club and kills the seal, or he puts up nets so that the seal cannot eat too many fish. His expectation is of lack—and his anxiety about his survival does not take into consideration that there is enough for everyone.

Be careful what you expect, for you may be driving someone too hard—yourself.

Aho.

# 7 ◆ FLOWERS AND ICE— COURAGE

I breathe in and out and I relax. I feel myself drifting deep, passing the physical brain and moving into the mind. Opening up my spirit eyes, I awake inside a lovely hut. Above me is a ceiling made of sticks. Light peers through the gaps, sunlight caresses my face. I sit up on a mat where I have been sleeping. My palette on the floor is made of different skins; coyote and wolf, otter, beaver, and buffalo. It is very soft and warm. There's a small fire on one side of the hut, a tiny fireplace, a small wooden table, a bookshelf with books, and that's it.

The hut is round and made from different kinds of sticks that are laced together and woven with grasses and herbs. Along the walls hang different bunches of dried flowers—honeysuckle, and roses of all colors and kinds. There's my favorite, the bitterroot rose, a small rose used to celebrate the birth of a child. The walls are layered with herbs—yarrow and clover, wild onion, rose hips, spearmint, sage, sweet grass, and bundles of cedar. The floor is made of different grasses woven together to make a rug.

It's quiet in the hut and very warm from the fire. I get up, put on my boots, lace them up, and open the door. It is snowing—deep snow.

Before me, the rushing creek is snaking its way through the ice. I put on my coat, hat, and gloves, gather my lizard bag and my medicine bundle and begin to cut a trail towards the creek. As I walk along, I see that winter is lightening up and beginning to taper off. Spring is not far away.

I look along the banks of the creek and see tiny flowers. Spirits emerge from the flowers, pink ones and green ones, yellow ones and orange ones, pale in color. They have wings. They flutter and spiral and dance in the day. I see their reflections in the water.

They are sweet spirits and remind me of my own Vision. They look a little like the seven stars dancing on the water in fairy form. I watch them as they spiral above the water and dart off, sparks in the air. They go in all directions. I feel the bright sun kiss my cheeks.

I hear a flock of geese overhead and the sound of someone speaking. I hear the word failure—an unusual thing to hear. Am I failing? Have I failed? Hmm . . .I haven't thought about failure since I was a young one and couldn't read like the English teacher wanted me to. I couldn't do my homework the way the teacher thought it should be done. I was made to feel inadequate in front of my peers and was often embarrassed.

As I stand in the North, I am beginning to understand that if we did not have such experiences, our spirit would never would never understand what it means to be imperfect or to make a mistake. We would not have the ability to have compassion.

I find a quiet spot beside a tree where it is dry, where the Sun has melted the snow. Pine needles make a soft comforting bed. I sit there among the tiny crocuses, the blue ones, the white ones, and my mind starts to drift. I shift into dream time and in front of me, I begin to see a dancer. Its colors are yellow and black. It spins around and around and around like a yellow and black tornado. I hear the drumbeat, and then I see clearly that it is a bumblebee dancer.

The dancer keeps spinning. He has a headpiece made of black feathers, and he has tied cloths onto his arms to make it appear as if he has wings. When he dances, he looks exactly like a bumblebee. He dances close to me and stops suddenly, kicking the dirt in the air.

"Good afternoon, Wolf. I am the Bee Dancer," and he nods. "I have come to you to speak about courage." He holds out his hand and gives me a gift of a huge bumblebee that is perfectly petrified. "That is the bumblebee and all the bees that represent Courage. We represent hard work. We also represent miracles, for I have heard that our wings are too small to lift our body off the ground, so we should not be able to fly," he says, "but we do."

"I know. I've heard that too," I reply. "You are truly a miracle, for your wings are small and your body's big."

"It is courage that makes that happen," he says with a smile. He has a beautiful young Native American face and long braids that are interlaced with black and yellow ribbon. He is dressed entirely in black and yellow and his moccasins are beaded in black and yellow, with bells on them. From his belt hang bells and black and yellow beads. When he spins, he buzzes. He is a total bumblebee.

The drumming gets loud again and he dances. One arm up and one arm down, he spins around. He looks as if he is flying. All around him, I see energy sparks and spirit beings—star people and fairies—they dance as he dances. He stops once more.

"You will be approached by a new apprentice. She is lost and the snabbers will try to steal her."

There's that word again. "What is a snabber anyhow?"

"Shh," he says. "You'll see soon enough and then you'll remember what it was like when the snabbers were after you. This will not be easy for you, but you must understand that this young one walks on the road of the lost soul. Her emptiness is because of the child abuse she experienced on Earth. There are many who suffer on their human two-legged walk. They suffer with diseases that come from chemical imbalances in their brain. They suffer from child abuse. They suffer from a lack of understanding, as you have."

His eyes are a piercing black and he has the most pleasant smile. I love his voice. "You must remember, Wolf, it's about courage. Courage medicine is what carries us across the river. It's what's brought you to the Blue-Eyed Raven. Congratulations, by the way," he smiles. "But your work is not over.

You must understand soul retrieval. You must help her, for her soul is lost. That means she has too many holes, holes, holes."

He becomes faint, I cannot see him well. He spins away in the dust.

I open my eyes and it is early evening. As I walk along the creek, I hear the sounds of geese flying north, as winter comes to an end. The spring thaw will start soon.

Ahead of me I hear familiar laughter, deep and friendly. I see a fire and two are sitting there. One is cloaked in a green blanket, and the other one I know is Dark Eyes. I see him, but I have no need to get closer to him. I have no yearning or passion, no romantic feelings. I have no desires, for I know who he is.

I take a deep breath of the cool evening air, the woods, and the pines. I hear the evening song of the owl, the hawk, the mockingbird, the whippoorwill. They are all coming home, getting into position to start their spring. As I walk closer, I hear the snapping of the fire and see the familiar camp, the buffalo roll, his home there by the river.

"I have never known anyone that I love so much," she says. "I love you, I want to stay here with you. I'll cut your wood."

"No, hush," he says. "You don't even know me." He shakes his head and runs his hands through his thick dark hair. "You're just running, kiddo. You're just trying to get away."

"No! No!" she says softly. "That's not true. I have not just come across this river by accident. I have found you. This is my home."

"So, you think that this is where you can stay forever?" he says.

She is fiddling with her hair, trying to tie two goose feathers into it.

"I have no place else to go, for I am a failure. I can't do anything but waitress work. I'm never going to get anywhere in this world. I want to stay with you. I know I love you. I can take good care of you."

"Well," he says, running his hands through his beard, "I guess we'll do it again."

"What do you mean?" she says.

"I guess I'll teach you. I guess I'll show you." He stands up and disappears in the dark.

She calls out his name. "Dark Eyes, you cannot leave me. Where have you gone?" She starts to follow him.

I step out and say, "No, don't go that way. There are those that wait for you."

She turns and looks at me. She is thin and long-legged, about 18 or 20 years old. She has beautiful brown hair with the goose feathers now tied into it.

"No, don't touch me," she says. "I don't know you. Go away." She is dressed in blue jeans and a flannel shirt. She is barefoot.

"I'm not going to hurt you. You can't chase him. You can't follow him. Wait!" I cry as she runs off.

I follow her into the night, into the darkness of the woods. We go deeper into the forest. It is cold. The night cloaks us in its emptiness and loneliness. I catch up with her and she is sitting on a rock, crying her eyes out.

I look at her and say, "What is the problem?"

"I must find him," she says. "I am nothing without Dark Eyes. He has asked me to dance in the moonlight with him."

"On the river," I say.

"What do you mean?" she looks at me, tears in her eyes. "Do you know his ways?

It dawns on me that I am in a new circle and Dark Eyes is now someone else's. It's her turn to dance by the river in the moonlight.

"No, I don't know his ways, but I can offer you one thing. You must have the medicine of Courage, and you must understand that maybe what you think is love and passion and romance is simply out-of-control emotions. You must be careful, or you will be trapped. You will be held against your will by your own feelings."

"You're jealous," she says. "You just want Dark Eyes for yourself. What would an old person like you want with someone so full of fire?" She spits at me and runs.

She gets quite a ways ahead of me, and I follow deep into the woods, deep into the night. I hear growls and hissing, low guttural sounds, muffled voices. I cannot make out what they're saying.

I move through the trees closer to the sounds. A fire is roaring bright and intense.

She stands encircled by ones with long fingernails, by dark figures dressed in willowy black with deep, glittering eyes.

"You must follow him and you must dance in the night," one says. "It is yours to cross the river with him. She, the one back there, is the one you must watch out for. She is filled with venom and will destroy your life. She haunts him and follows him, wishing to engulf him."

"Yes, that's what she does," says another in a squeaky voice. "She will never let him go, for she is eaten up with jealousy. Listen to us, and we will teach you the ways of the woman. You must be filled with hate, for she has come to destroy your love. She will take him away from you."

They all begin to speak at once and sing, weaving the words back and forth. It is a simple melody. They dance around her, around the fire.

109

"See her for what she is, the one who wants to take him from you. Understand that a woman must be filled with courage and stand on her own. She must stand up to anyone who tries to take her man. He is yours."

I know that these are Snabbers. I know they are the thoughts of greed and envy, of jealousy, and ownership. How will she ever find the courage to break away? How will she know that she is facing the lesson of failure? They sway and dance around her, and the wind blows the goose feathers from her hair. They fall to the dirt.

"You will never fail," one of them says. "You are strong in your own empowerment. You are a woman, and he is yours."

They take off their gowns and dance naked, swaying and weaving around her with their long scraggly black hair, cavernous eyes, and gaunt faces. They dance shadows around the fire.

"You are the real woman."

Two of them hold onto her and say, "What are your feelings? Do you feel the anger? Do you feel the pain that she is going to cause you? You must strike like a snake."

They hiss and growl.

"How can I tell her to have courage? How can I show her that they are Snabbers? Now I know them. They are run-away emotions. She must see that to find her soul mate, she has to break free from their lies and torment."

Now there are hundreds of Snabbers. They are coming from every direction, spewing poison and fear, telling her that he is hers, telling her that she is to own him and have all that she ever wanted in life.

I start to walk away and I hear the crying of young girls. I heard the crying of young children everywhere.

"Stop!" I cry out. I turn around and look at her. "Let me tell you about the bumblebee. It is a miracle. Its wings are too small, but it flies anyhow because it has courage and dignity. Walk the Rainbow Path. Follow the teachings of the Rainbow Medicine Wheel. Look beyond this. Call out to your Grandmother/Grandfather Wolf/Great Spirit. Do not settle for Snabbers. Do not let them torment you! There is more to life than Dark Eyes—you'll see. Dark Eyes is nothing more than the South, nothing more than King Coyote, the one who holds you hostage. You must break free and find your soul mate. You must live your life, as I have."

She looks at me in torment and anguish. She drops her head and begins to weep.

"Listen to me. Don't allow your emotions to devour you. You are in a deep lesson, the lesson of failure. Emotions can make us feel as if we have failed. In the spirit realm there is enlightenment, and in the emotions there needs to be trust and innocence. In the body there is introspection—the ability to go within the self and understand. You are not alone."

A Snabber grabs me and digs its nails into my shoulder, wrenching me around.

"Listen to me," she growls. "No, she is not alone. She is ours. She is the soul of darkness that we have chosen to torment. She is the child of all children. She is the way that we please to distort the minds of those that walk as two-leggeds on this Earth. The lies will remain."

The old spirit is haggard and worn. Her hair is twisted and tangled; her eyes have blood around them. Her nose is flared, and her teeth are rotted. She gives out a foul smell.

"Get your hands off me," I say. "I will send you back where you came from." I extend my hand and light springs out from the ends of my fingers. It coats her and turns her into Beauty. She becomes a lovely young woman, going for a walk in the woods. She passes us by. I turn back to the young girl I had been speaking to.

"Listen to me and do not get caught up in lies. Turn and walk away now. What is it that makes you come to him in the first place but a lonely soul? I see your soul and know that it is broken. I know it has holes in it. I know that there are energy leaks, and I know that you are in trouble, but that is only because you have walked on the earth and forgotten who you are spiritually. Let me show you."

I point to the right and extend my fingers and colored stars shoot forth. A young woman stands before me with her arms around a handsome young man. They dance together by the river.

"No one will ever love me," she cries. "I am a total loss, a total failure."

The Snabbers' energy grows stronger. They begin come out from behind the trees and underneath the rocks and head toward the girl.

I hear a hissing, a growling, and a horrible rasping sound.

"Stop it!" I call out. "You must stop speaking of yourself that way. All humans have days when they lose their courage and cannot walk. All humans believe they are frail like flowers that come out at the start of the spring—the time of ice and flower, the beginning. You are at the doorway of Spring—the East."

She looks at me and says, "You know?"

"Yes," I tell her. "I have suffered as a human. I've been tested to the limit. I've lost, I've faced death. I've felt alone and anguished, but I have followed the Rainbow Path, and I've listened to Grandmother/Grandfather/Great Spirit, and I've held hope in my heart. It is the inner Strength of Prayer that we walk with. It is knowing that one can rise from the dead. If you allow these tormenters to come to you, King Coyote will simply take you with him, feed on your Strength, and forget you exist, for he is the ultimate of all emotions. Your emotions will never betray you if you have Strength and make the medicine of Understanding and knowing number one in your heart. Listen for the Will of Great Spirit."

**I hear the howl of the wolf calling me back.**

## THE TEACHINGS OF COURAGE— BEE MEDICINE

It is in the North section of the wheel that each human being finds the answers to why he or she exists. Each human is its brain, and the brain is the home of the mind, and the mind is the home of the soul. Within the brain, the thoughts of the mind bring forth the Understanding of life.

Everything in the human body is powered by the brain. Today we are close to the answers of the secrets of death and sickness. As we accept that a healthy brain is the answer to all illness, we will be open to the thoughts of our mind. When we think healthy thoughts, we live a truly spiritual life.

Our brain has many diseases and traumas that slow us down and impair our lifestyle. I see mental health as the doorway to good living and fun memories. We, as humans, make our own Choice to be healthy or unhealthy.

I think of emotions simply as reactions. I have the ability to have acceptance. I have the ability to have disgust. I have the ability to be sad or happy. I have the ability to be angry or to have fear or joy. Those are the seven primary emotions.

One of the most common brain disorders is post-traumatic stress. Many people think it comes only when someone's been in the war. This isn't true. People suffer from post-traumatic stress all over the world, because fear pushes the synapse process to the point where stress produces severe depression.

Now, what I am teaching you is about Courage, and Courage is getting up like the flowers that come through the snow in the early spring. As we live our lives every day, every human being is faced with the opportunity to use Courage. Courage is a medicine that allows you stand up and find the truth.

When you are in the deepest, darkest part of your despair, you're close to being destroyed. If you can get yourself up by talking to people, that's Courage. If you can do it through Prayer, that's Courage. If you can do it by seeking out a psychologist and getting counseling, that's Courage. Going to AA meetings or NA meetings is Courage. The ultimate Courage is seeking out a neurologist or a psychiatrist and finding out if you have a severe mental disorder, because you need to find a way to stop your suffering. You can not just go along from one day to the next hoping you'll feel better sometime. Through all the ceremonies, and all the medicines, there are answers, but Courage is the major one. It is the green one that stands out. It is the Growth that brings about the Beauty that brings changes to your life.

Courage is bravery. It is grand-hearted. It is gallant, it is fearless, it is bold, it is fortitude and endurance. None of those words are weak. We lose people every day because they give up, believing that they are weak. You are not weak. You're just not listening to your mind. You are not connecting to the spiritual voice that comes through your thoughts saying that you need help. We have parents or grandparents or aunts and uncles, or good friends, and the possibility of getting good advice in our lives.

Giving up is the opposite of Courage. Courage is one of the strongest medicines in the medicine wheel. Is your soul damaged? Do you have problems in balancing your chakras? Do you need to go inside and journey and find the answers?

When I spoke to the bewildered girl, I advised her properly. She can face the King Coyote—that is all her emotions—and so can you. Hate is an emotion, and love is an emotion; bitterness is an emotion. Courage is a medicine you can apply to your life that gets you through those emotions. All you have to do is have Courage.

Remember Job in the Bible? Everything was taken away from him. This happens when people lose their child. This happens when someone's half-side dies too soon. This happens when we become co-dependent, and when we think that we need possessions, such as cars and houses. With Courage, we make the Choice to get help and be all we can be. There are many who can help us. All we have to do is find the right person.

Aho.

# CEREMONY OF COURAGE

**Tools:** *Seven candles in different shades of green; blue cornmeal, 1-2 pounds (If you can not find blue, use white cornmeal); candle holders; smudging supplies; your journal and pen.*

You can perform this Ceremony any time you need to feel the circle of Courage. The words of Courage are brave, grand-hearted, gallant, fearless, bold, fortitude, and endurance. Connect one of the green candles to each one of those words. Each one of the candles must be a different shade of green—pale green, yellow green, spring green, mint green, dark green, and any other shades of green that you can find.

It is important to connect the candles to the words. Do it by writing the word down and placing a candle beside it. Once you have connected each candle to a different word, see which of the words are connected to the palest colored candles. The palest colored words are the strongest words in your life at the moment. The words next to the darker candles are the ones you need to be concerned about. They are the weak spots within your Courage.

Go to a quiet place where you can draw seven lines on the ground with cornmeal. The Ceremony is best done outside where you can put the cornmeal down as a give-away to the Earth. This will strengthen your connection with the Earth Mother as she brings forth an Understanding of your medicine teachings.

You will need to smudge first. Do this by lighting sage, blowing out the fire, and letting the smoke rise and drift around the area before you do the ceremony. When you are finished smudging, let the smoke continue to rise till you are done with the Ceremony. Then put the fire out.

Draw a line with the cornmeal three feet (1m) wide. After you have drawn it, stand with your heels touching it and walk forward. Pace off three feet—one big step—and repeat the process, drawing another three-foot wide line on the ground. Then take another giant step and place a line, until you have seven cornmeal lines on the ground where you can see them.

Go back to the first line, open your journal and write the word "brave." Beneath it, make a note that you need to look up the word in the dictionary and understand what it means and how to apply it to your life. As you cross each line, write down the word that is connected with it (page 115) and make a note that you need to know the definition and how to apply it to your life.

As you come to each line, place the candle that you have connected to the word at the line. Start with the first line, "brave," and light the candle. Then step to the next line and light the candle. Do the same until you get to the seventh word. When you have lit the candle of "endurance," walk back up the lines about midway and sit down.

Look at the lines and understand they go in the order of this teaching. What do I do to be brave? How am I grand-hearted? When do I need to be gallant? Why do I need to be fearless? What do I do to show my boldness? How do I have fortitude? Why do I need to have endurance?

Sit with these questions and answer them in your journal. Also give examples of any of the seven words of Courage that you have displayed in your life over the years. Journal acts in your life of bravery, grand-heartedness, gallantry, fearlessness, boldness, fortitude, and endurance. Journal about how you can take a circumstance in your life today and apply your new-found Courage.

To apply courage, you need to understand the circle of Courage, the seven words within it, how, why, and when to apply them—and what to apply them to.

After you have written in your journal, decide how long you are going to work on Courage. Will it take a day, a week, a month? Set a time for each day, or each week, or each month to come back to the lines and light the candles as you learn more about what your bravery is, what your endurance is, and the rest. When you feel that you understand Courage and what it takes to stand on your own, facing the fact that you have a human brain and must open up to your mind, snuff out the candles. Give the cornmeal away to the earth with a Prayer, remembering that you understand Courage and have Courage in your life.

It is a good thing to sit at your Courage Ceremony at sunrise, at noon, at sunset, and at midnight to feel your thoughts of Courage all around the circle of the Day.

Aho.

## THE LESSON OF FAILURE—
## GOOSE MEDICINE

Fear is the main reason why we fail. There are other things that can help us fail, such as:

1. A lack of learning.

2. Not understanding the action at hand.
3. Not knowing what you need to be doing.
4. Not being in the right place at the right time.
5. Not having the training you need to do what you wish to do.
6. Not having enough money.
7. Having brain damage and being unable to learn.
8. Not setting goals.
9. Not studying enough.
10. Not understanding or knowing the rules of the topic.

All of these are reasons why you might fail. The important lesson of failure is that it is a doorway—the doorway to success and the opportunity to have Success. Opportunity is the key. When you learn the lesson, you will see that you can start over any time you want. The school of hard knocks will teach you to think things through before you start on a project in life.

The biggest reason we, as humankind, fail is that we don't know what lies ahead. We rush into action because we see others doing it and think we should keep up with them. To learn the lesson of failure, you need to give yourself the opportunity to plan and set goals. Journal your actions. If you find that you will not do the paperwork and that you are suffering from overwhelm, you need help. You need to check your mental health and make sure your brain is working right. That means getting your chemicals checked and making sure you are well mentally. You might have an imbalance in your diet, or your sugars might be off, or you might be affected by the use of alcohol or drugs. You might be lacking in proper sleeping habits, or exercise. There might also be a lack of Prayer and spiritual work. Always know you can apply the medicines of the Rainbow Medicine Wheel and make Changes in your life.

## GOOD THINGS TO DO
## WHEN YOU FAIL OR FEEL YOU ARE A FAILURE

1. Start over.
2. Make new friends.
3. Forget and forgive.
4. Study and learn more.
5. Seek out help.
6. Speak to your guides.

7. Be open to opportunity.
8. See everything as an adventure and know you will be able to overcome all things.
9. Have faith.
10. Have goals and plans. Check the goals and make changes in your plans.
11. Seek out a psychiatrist or psychologist, minister, shaman, or other spiritual teacher. Seek counsel from your elders.
12. Have a regular Prayer time. Pray and write in your journal, expressing any anger and unbalanced emotions.
13. Go for a walk or to the movies; play a game, or spend time with children or pets.
14. Spend time at your altar or in the medicine wheel.

The totem for failure is the goose. It knows when to leave. There is a saying that goes with this lesson: "Don't stay too long and don't leave too soon." Geese move South for the winter and North for the summer. Because they move at the right time, the one that suits the season, there is no dislike of where they are, no unhappiness, and no failure. They will always have food and survive. Remember that, as the lesson of failure happens, you will come to a place where everything in your life is an opportunity.

Aho!

## ACTIONS TO OVERRIDE FAILURE

Working in a journal, making personal tapes, and listening to them are some of the best things you can do when you wish not to fail. Everything in the human two-legged life is set up in terms of learning.

It is very important to understand your individual qualities when you're working with failure. When you don't take time to understand brain damage or mental health, for example, you are acting foolishly. When you don't consult your elders or listen to the healers, you are setting yourself up for failure. You only fail when you do not know that you are fallible. Being able to spell and read and count is the way of the world, but having stamina, being creative, and bringing forth Growth and Beauty, are the important qualities to be learned from the lesson of Failure.

*Exercise*: In your journal, answer the following questions.

1. Where do you feel you are a failure? How did it happen and how does

it continue to happen?
2. When you think of things you need to do in life, what can you not do? Why can't you do it and when will you learn to do it?
3. Are there things in life that you feel you couldn't do if you had to? List them. Why do you feel this way? How long have you felt this way and when will you change it?
4. When you think of spirit, do you know that you are a spirit? Can you see and speak with spirits? If not, why not, and when are you going to change that?
5. Why do you like to fail? Why do you like to be in denial and say that you don't fail? Who sets up failing in your life? Why? When are you going to change things?

These questions will help you see how you interact with your failures and how you interact with failing. I use the word "denial," because it's important not to pretend or deny, or lie to yourself about who you are. When you look at your problems, be they health issues or money issues, or alcohol substance issues, or chronic drug use issues, you can get to the bottom of how you feel by asking yourself questions about failure.

You have the freedom to understand the lesson of failure and see that only you can cause yourself to fail. You may need some counseling and even medicine from a doctor (a psychiatrist) to make it through the issues that have been dealt you by your genes and the teachings that you have endured. But getting those needs met is in your hands.

A true failure is when we hurt ourselves or another. Many times as humankind we hurt ourselves or set others up to hurt us. A true failure is when we take our life or another's. We as humankind are hard on ourselves and others, and it is a good thing when learning the lesson of failure to look at the reason we're failing or have failed, and see if it is our Choice or someone's else's expectations. We have the right to be ourselves, and sometimes that is not what others think we should be. Remember that failure is a lesson, and the lesson is learned when we know what is expected of us and decide whether we want to live up to the expectation. Also remember that Great Spirit wants for you only what you can do. A failure is an opportunity.

Aho.

# 8 ◆ TEARS IN THE RIVER—UNDERSTANDING MEDICINE

I breathe in and out, and the cold air around me is crisp and fresh. I love to walk in the spirit world, to be home by the river. I stop and listen. I hear the wind. I hear the owl. I hear the birds singing their songs, the ones who are returning from the South. I see the seagull overhead.

I have followed the river where it enters into the sea. I step out into a coved area. I feel very tired and very cold. I have walked a long time. I kneel down, and place my bundle on the ground in front of me. I carry the lizard bundle in great anticipation of seeing the face of Great Spirit/Creator soon. I will find the place that Grandmother/Grandfather Wolf wish me to go. I reflect on the young one who has turned to Dark Eyes, to the weak ones who need someone to support them, to the ones who run from the Snabbers, and I think about how they are like the students who enter the lodge.

They are all looking, looking for answers, looking for memories, looking for the path. I touch the lizard bundle and watch the sun set in the ocean. The snow is deep and the ice kisses the shoreline. I guess this is my place for the night. It's funny how even in spirit, we can feel cold.

Sometimes I can't understand, when I'm in the spirit world, why heat is so important and why we have to eat. I would have thought that would all be behind us. There is so much to understand, but I know that all I have to do is call out and the answers will come.

I look at the early night sky and see one solitary star. I must find a place to rest. I see a cave back in the depths of the cove. I walk that way. As I approach the entrance to the cave, I see a huge starfish lying on the ground. It must have been left behind when the tide moved out. I pick it up and hold it in my hand. It glows with a beautiful blue light.

The starfish is still alive, so I start to run for the water, but a voice says, "Stop! Don't go there, bring it here. It will teach you Understanding."

An old woman is standing in the cave. She is holding a walking stick made from driftwood. On it are all types of sea urchins, sea horses, and starfish, other shells, rocks with holes in it, and interesting pieces of wood, and sticks.

She is a tall, thin, beautiful older woman. Her hair is silver and pulled back in a ponytail. Her face is round and slightly wrinkled, but you can see her age. She is wearing a coat made from a striped blanket. It is a medicine coat, for on the front are small medicine bundles and ribbons in different shades of blue and turquoise laced on.

The bottom of the coat is fringed, and there are pieces of small driftwood on it, and rocks with holes, and other beautiful shells that match the walking stick. As I get closer, I see that half her face changes to a star—half of a star—exactly like the starfish I hold in my hand.

"Ahh, heya, Starlight star bright, first star I see tonight. The star is that of the white wind, the wolf," she says and smiles.

She has clear blue eyes and a dimple on her left cheek. As I get closer, I notice an exquisite necklace of aquamarine stones. "Welcome, welcome, Wolf. Come in and bring the starfish of Understanding."

A river of water is running along the side of the cave. As we walk in, she says, "Place the starfish there in that water and it will be fine. It is salt water."

I lay the starfish back in the water and I notice that there are hundreds of them lining the bottom of the river. They are all different colors—reds, burgundies, purples, blues, and some were green. The cave wall is all crystal in colors of aquamarine, pale purples, and pale blues, with huge crystal spears. Some are a hundred feet (30m) tall coming up out of the ground and the sides of the cave.

The cave is warm and dry and a huge bonfire is glistening in the stones and reflecting the warmth. This is her home. There are all types of driftwood—her furniture is made of driftwood, too, and magnificent conch shells and turtle shells line the walls.

It is wonderful to walk about among the different sea creatures and the dramatic driftwood. There are old boats that she has turned into beds.

"You're welcome to stay here, Wolf. I know where you're heading and you're right on the path," she says quickly. "Let me fix you some supper," she smiles—and I know.

"It's one of those awful tasting meals that Grandmother Wolf wants me to try, right?"

She says, "Well, I'll be real honest with you. It's octopus."

"Hmm," I say. "Do I have to?"

She says, "I think you'll find it good—a little fishy, but you'll like it."

She lifts the lid of the pot that is on the old wood stove. "Yeah, it washed up on shore one day. I guess it was coming in on a boat, might have fallen off," she says.

She stirs the soup.

"Yeeaah," I take a whiff and it is really fishy. "But, there's probably a reason, right?"

"Yes," and she sticks out her hand and shakes it at me. "I am the Starfish One," she says. "I walk with Understanding of the mysteries and I know the path well enough to tell you where the door is that leads to the land of the 28 moons. That is the place where you will see the face, where you can look for the echo of life and hear the Will of Great Spirit/ Creator/God."

She sets the table, puts some porridge bowls down, and makes a salad of sea greens. When she spoons some soup into my bowl, I don't waste any time—I just drink it.

"Wow! Yuck! How fishy can it get?"

"Oh," she says with a smile, "it's good for you. It'll cleanse and restore your soul."

"Oohh, if I don't die first," and I shake my head, quivering from side to side. "Bluh."

I wipe my mouth with the back of my hand and say, "Why is it that my Grandfather and Grandmother's friends have to have food that tastes so bad?"

"Here," she puts another spoon in. "Eat this."

I sniff this soup and it smells wonderful—like mushrooms—like fresh mushroom soup. I scarf it right down.

"Ymm, wow, that's good. May I have some more please?"

She walks over and puts the spoon in the same pot where the horrible tasting octopus soup came from.

"Uh, no. I want the mushroom."

She draws up the soup, brings it back, sets it down and says, "Smell."

I take a whiff, and it is the wonderful mushroom soup. She looks at me and says, "No, it's octopus. It's what you think that makes something what it is. Do you think a starfish is a star, or do you think it is a fish?"

I say, "It's a fish."

"It's a star," she says. She points to the water where the starfish are and they glisten and sparkle. Stars—there are so many, the ground looks like the sky.

"There, Wolf. There is the doorway."

I look at her and say, "Through the ground? I must go to the lower world to find the face of the Creator?"

"It's kind of like the octopus soup. Everything that goes down is not always in the lower world, for you go in and out. You're going out there."

I turn, and there is a cave door.

"Go beyond. You'll see a white staircase made of stars. The stars are diamonds. They glisten and sparkle and shine. The color will be intense. Climb them and go beyond, and you will know you're there by the way the lights hit the Earth. Twenty-eight moons in seven sets of fours in colors you will not forget, and soon you will see what you want. There you will find the Will and you will teach of Will and stand in the beginning again."

I take a deep breath in and out. I find myself walking a silver path. I hear the waves crashing on the shore.

Before me, I see a path. It is very inviting. I hear birds singing. I walk on that path and the trees begin to talk.

"Does she know of Understanding?" one says.

"Has anybody told her about Understanding?" another one says.

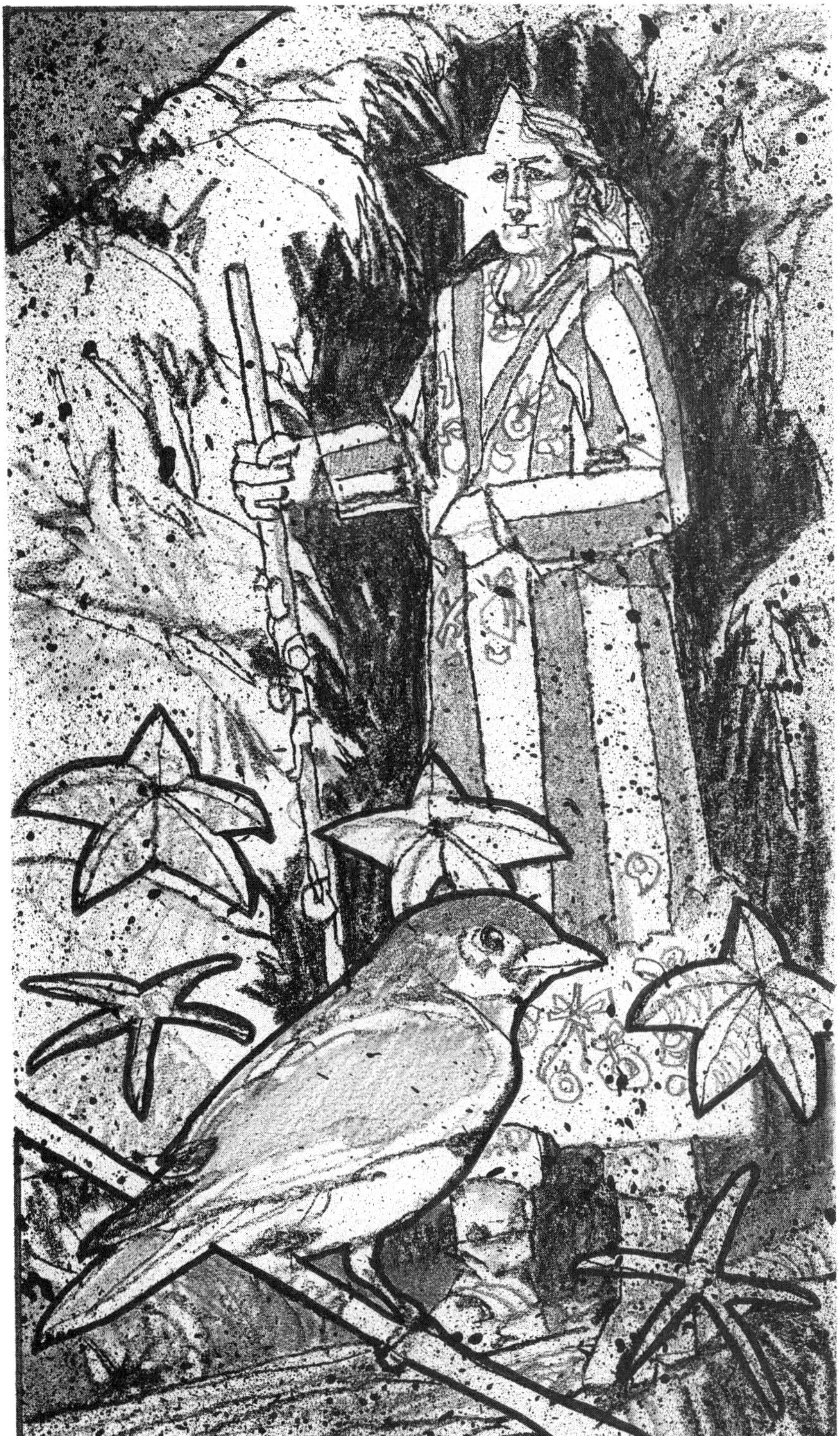

"She must know of Understanding," says another.

I come to a gigantic cedar.

"Hello," the tree says. "I am Grandmother Cedar. Has anyone told you about Understanding? Do you really comprehend it?"

The tree must be close to 200 feet (60m) tall. I bend my neck completely back to look at. It seems to go on forever. It is beautiful and fragrant.

"I will tell you of Understanding, for it is an important medicine. I would like to think of it as the starfish medicine," it says, "because it is what the teacher of starfish has blessed you with—Understanding. It is comprehension. It is intelligence. It is Knowledge. It is cooperation and agreement, interpretation, and grasp. And, it is all in your future, Wolf. Soon you will have walked the whole medicine wheel. You will have an understanding of the spirit, the emotions, the body, and the mind. Then, you will have Responsibility. It is Sweet Medicine—being able to walk ahead—being able to stand in your center."

The voice of the cedar tree circles through my mind and opens my thoughts to Understanding. I walk on in the lush forest. There are ferns, bird songs that I have never heard before. The path is made of pine needles and cedar. As I walk, I can tell I am climbing. I am going higher. I reach the top, and look out over the ocean. It goes on to infinity. There is a stillness on the mountaintop. Everything is quiet.

"Interpretation," I hear from a very tiny voice. "Interpretation, that is what the mind does. The mind is a recording bank. It is for humankind to know the reason of the humankind. They must interpret. They must look deep into the soul and understand spirit life, their memories of the spirit world, or the struggle in their minds. When humankind listen, they can hear their spiritual truths," the voice says.

It is a beautiful little bluebird speaking.

"And who are you?" I ask the little bird.

"I am the lesson of listening," it says in a soft voice. "I think you need to know whether you listen. Do you listen? Often humankind hears—when they want to have their way. But they need to listen so that they can hear. It is not what they're thinking that they should listen to, but what is. When you listen to what you are thinking, you are hearing your thoughts and demanding your way, but to truly listen is to hear spirit. Then you are on the path of Knowing. Listening is easy. When you learn the lesson of listening, then you know your soul."

"Soul. Yes, that's interesting. I've always wanted to know about the soul. Are you the one to teach me?"

"I don't know. I don't know if they'll let me tell you about that or not.

Sometimes the soul is a learning that we find on our own. All the teachers before me have done a good job telling you of the soul.

"The important thing is that you must remember your way to Grandfather/Grandfather/Great Spirit. You must listen to the Grandfather part of the story, and then you must feel the Grandmother part of the story. Grandfather/Grandmother/Great Spirit want you to share with your students the true teachings of Will. It is important for them that their souls are strong, for that's how they get here. It is important that they remember the Beauty of the seven colored birds on the earth. Everything is seven colors," the bluebird says. "Everything in history has seven colors—everything except fear and anguish, and anger. They turn everything dark and gray. They make it dismal. They forget the colors, and they go deep into mental illness."

"Illness, illness," echoes in my mind. I hear it over and over again. "Interpretation, interpretation," and I awaken sitting against the wall in the lodge.

**I hear the howl of the wolf calling me back.**

## THE TEACHINGS OF UNDERSTANDING— STARFISH MEDICINE

I like to say that Understanding is the glue that holds things together in Life. When you Understand, you are safe, well-adjusted, able, and have the ability to achieve your goals. The starfish is the totem for Understanding. The starfish is simple and has Beauty. It is full of Mystery, but it is clear that it is a fish and has a purpose—to be.

As you use the Medicine of Understanding, it brings Beauty to your life. It is listening to spirit. When you understand, you are listening to your soul.

Understanding is a personal medicine. You can have an Understanding, and the people right next to you have no Understanding of their lives at all.

We each see what we want and have the Understanding that we need to learn from. For example, a starfish looks like a star, and that is the shape you see. But it is not a star, it is a fish. To one person it is a star, to another, a fish.

Understanding is comprehension. To be able to comprehend you need a healthy brain and an open mind. You need to listen with your mind—not with what many call the heart. The heart is the blood pump in our physical body: it does *not* think. When people say they think with their heart, they are speaking from confusion. What they mean is that they are thinking with feeling—with emotion, not just reacting.

We do not think with our gut, either, or "feel it in our gut." When you have a gut feeling, you are feeling the emotion of fear, and you need to think things through better—or listen to your fear and make the best Choice. All thinking happens from the mind through the brain.

We need to use the right words when we talk with children about these things. It is hard enough to learn the lessons of Life, without using confusing terms. We need to get to the point.

Understanding is intelligence. To have and be intelligent means the brain must be healthy and working properly. To have the brain work in the right way, we need to be born with a healthy brain, have good eating habits, and good rest and sleep habits, along with the proper chemical balance.

It is intelligent—when you suffer or see someone else suffer—to seek help from your elders, healers, doctors, or shamans. It is a wise idea to seek the counsel of more than one elder.

Understanding is agreement. When you agree with something, you feel it. You know it is the right thing for you to do. You can also disagree with something and agree that it is not for you. But, if you have anger or unresolved issues, it is hard to come to any kind of agreement.

Agreement is the flow within a Choice. To agree you need to research the facts and know the goals at hand.

One person's truth is another's lie. You must have the background and the facts. Always check out a teaching from many sides and with many people before you come to agreement.

Understanding is very important medicine. Motive, values, and belief play a strong part in it. We don't always understand the faith of our Life, but with time come answers, with answers comes Understanding. As you walk with Understanding, you will see that the physical part of the self is the brain, the spirit part of the self is the mind, and our soul is made up of the paths we take in our pure Energy form—all of our total existence.

Aho!

# CEREMONY OF THE SOUL

**Tools:** *1 pound of white cornmeal; 7 colored candles: red, orange, yellow, green, blue, purple, and burgundy; a white candle and a silver candle; a jar of silver glitter; journal and pen.*

The Ceremony of the Soul is a way to connect and have a symbol with which to understand your soul. I like to teach about the soul as the connection between your physicality and your spirituality. In my Vision long ago, I remember Grandmother/Grandfather/Great Spirit dropping me down to the earth on a silver cord, much as a spider would spin a cord and drop off the web. That silver cord never let go of me. It was attached through the umbilical cord of my mother.

When my mother cut the cord—that is, when I became physical—I still was connected with my silver cord and am to this day to Grandmother/Grandfather/Great Spirit. The silver cord is the way I go home, for it is a shimmering path of Color that glistens and glitters. I will climb it and find my way back. That is my daily life. As I walk back on the Good Red Road of Life, I am climbing the silver cord, walking on my soul.

It is important that your soul does not get snagged, or thin. These actions can happen when you're mentally ill, when your emotions are out of balance. When you suffer from rage or passion, or follow the romantic roads in life, when you have greed for money or envy of others, or are jealous, when you suffer from uncontrollable desires—that can weaken you in spirit. The Ceremony of the Soul allows you to strengthen yourself, to have Understanding. It is important for you, as a human, for your soul to be strong, for your path to be intact, so that you can climb your way to the spirit world.

This Ceremony is to be done in bright sunlight between 12 and 3 o'clock any day of the week.

Go to a quiet place where you can draw a circle in cornmeal. You can do this outside in the dirt or inside. Outside is best.

First, smudge the area, by lighting the sage or sweet grass, blowing the fire out, and fanning the smoke over the area to clean it of negative Energy.

Then draw a circle—a large circle—on the ground with the cornmeal. Set the seven candles in fireproof candleholders clockwise in a circle, starting on the right side of the circle with red and going on to orange, yellow, green , blue, purple, and burgundy. Make a complete circle out of the candles. Take your silver glitter and starting in the center of the circle, pour a glitter line to the North, crossing the circle line and going 14 inches

(35cm) outside the circle. Then place a white candle in the center of the circle. This represents Creator, where all things come from. Place the silver candle next to the white one to represent the soul and the silver cord.

Make sure you place your candles in fireproof candleholders.

Then, to find the understanding of your soul, take out your pen and journal the answers to the following questions, with four answers each.

1. What do you comprehend? List four things that you understand. It is important to understand what you comprehend in life.

> **Example:** *A simple example of this is what color your hair is, or what color your eyes are. Your comprehension may be that people are wrong and bad, or that people are basically good and you can see the positive aspects in everyone. More complex would be why you exist, what your spiritual beliefs are.*
>
> Give four answers to what you comprehend.

2. What are your intelligences? There are many different types of intelligence. Give four facts.

> **Example:** *You are artistic. You can draw, sing, dance, and act. You have a great ability to read, study, comprehend information and share it with others. You may have an aptitude for sewing and crafts, or painting, or automotives and mechanics, or cooking or music. Your intelligence could even be watching TV—understanding and grasping it—or being able to play trivia games, or work a crossword puzzle without help, or have the ability to find your niche in life.*

3. What Knowledge do you have? What are you knowledgable about? Everything that we know is a part of Great Spirit.
Give four answers.

> **Example:** *You can do multiplication tables, you know that the sun will come up tomorrow and that defines daytime. It could be something as simple as knowing how to stack matches and make a match house, or knowing how to ride a bike.*

4. What do you cooperate with? Your cooperation's show how you fit into your community. Give four answers.

> **Example:** *You can play music in a band and you cooperate with the*

*others to make the music come forth. It could be how you share your feelings with other people in a good way.*

5. What agreements do you have? Your "agreements" are the ones where you hold strong on what's right and wrong—where you understand a topic and are clear about what you are to do within it.

Cite four agreements.

> **Example:** *People can agree to disagree, meaning that a child can say it doesn't like spinach, and its parents will still accept it and love it. One person likes blue and another person likes yellow. They both like Color but each has its own particular Color he or she likes.*

6. What actions do you see taking place in your life?

You work with shamanic Journeys and seek out answers for the journeys. You have a regular prayer time and make prayer. You study your medicine words: Color, Energy, Prayer, Courage, Understanding, Knowledge, and Will. You study the Lessons in your life—trust, limits, life, failure, listening, forgiveness, and inner peace. You apply Knowledge to your life daily from your study of these words.

Cite four actions.

> **Example:** *You have a shamanic journey and you see yourself forgiving a person who has harmed you. You come back to normal thinking and journal the vision. You then go to work setting up a meeting with someone who has caused you harm. You apply Courage to your actions, face the person and tell him or her how you feel.*

7. What responsibilities do you have? If you have something it is yours to take care of. Care is the key word in responsibilities. If you do not want responsibilities then do not have thing and stuff, friends and family. Your responsibilities in life reveal not only the things you hold onto but the things that hold onto you.

> **Example:** *Children—you can't just leave them and go anywhere you want any time you want. Your pets need attention—you can't just tie them up and leave them. Your home needs care and cleaning, you can't just walk off and let it go.*

Give four examples.

When you answer these seven questions with four sets of answers, you will begin to have an understanding of your personality. If you can answer all the questions, then you are strong and are guided by a solid walk within your soul. If you have a hard time answering them, it's time for you to figure out why you are so despondent, so detached, and so disconnected from yourself.

After you have answered the questions, turn to the Ceremony and light the red candle reflecting on your comprehensions. Light the orange candle and reflect on your intelligences. Light the yellow candle and reflect on your Knowledge. Light the green candle, and reflect on your cooperations; the blue candle, your agreements; the purple candle, your interpretations, and for the burgundy candle, reflect on your responsibilities.

After you have lit all seven candles, light the center candle reflecting on the energy of Great Spirit/Creator/God. With a firm understanding of your connection with this energy, light the silver candle, knowing that the silver path is the cord that connects you to Great Spirit/Creator/God. Understand that the silver line reflects your soul. If your soul seems weak, you will find the reason in one of the answers that you have given to the questions.

When you finish the Ceremony and feel strong in your soul, make sure the line of glitter is strong. Blow out the candles in a counter-clockwise direction, starting with the last candle you set down. Place the candles someplace that they'll be safe so that you can use them again if you need to. Gather up the cornmeal and scatter it on the Earth for the Crawlies and those that come to celebrate the Ceremony of Soul. Take your glitter and blow it from your hand in places that you feel are good representations of you and your walk on the Earth Mother. This could be such places as at the seashore, in the park, in the city, at a shopping center, in a forest, in the desert—any place that reflects who you are. Take some of the glitter and blow it there.

Understand that the silver cord connects you with Grandmother/Grandmother/Great Spirit/Creator/God and that in all things that your soul is strong and diverse.

Aho.

## THE LESSON OF LISTENING— THE BLUEBIRD

When you are learning the lesson of listening, there are needs to be met. It is very important to be listened to. It affects your Color, Energy and Knowledge. Listening is being able to move to a new level of being. When you learn to listen, you gain Understanding from the Knowledge you obtain. To learn the lesson of listening, you must focus on what the person is saying and what his or her goals are—not what you want the person to say to make your life easy. You gain from listening because you know where you stand in the speaker's life. Whether you are listening to a humankind or spirit, it is important to hear what the speaker is saying.

When you seek a smooth life and wish to listen, you need to apply humility in your life. Being grateful and respectful of others and their thoughts shows you are listening. You do not have to agree with others, but you do need to respect their ways and understand their needs.

When you are angry or filled with rage or hate, you are not be able to hear the person who is speaking, and you will miss the point.

To learn this lesson, you need to practice the medicine of the bluebird. The bluebird is known for happiness and modesty, for its simple life and Beauty that affects every person who sees it. It arouses great joy. Its life is one of fulfillment. When you are around the bluebird, it soothes your worries. It is the same with the lesson of listening. When you have listened, you will come to know what you need to do or what your Choice is, and you can make a an intelligent decision.

As you learn the lesson of listening, you can apply the medicine of Understanding. The medicine will give you Success and Truth. When you understand anything you are Committed. You make a Choice and follow the way of the Choice. In each action in your life you either understand what you are doing or you follow blindly. When understanding is the Choice you make, you will have goals and a plan. The outcome will be Success.

There is great Success in the lesson of listening, for you will receive the words of your Vision. A Vision or Ceremony is heard as well as seen. To bring it forth, you must learn to listen, which means hearing the way it is—not the way you want it to be. For example, you look in the sky and you see a cloud that looks like a woman—an old woman—but you say to yourself it is only clouds. Or you hear a voice that tells you it is an ancestor speaking to you, but you say no—it's a cloud—and walk off and do not see the rest of the Vision or hear the other words to come. To learn to listen, we must believe what we see and hear.

Aho.

# 9 ◆ WALKING THE RIVER—KNOWLEDGE MEDICINE

Tonight I see each student in that place in purple where they begin to understand. This group is strong. They have come a long way and they have studied hard, and now they stand in the North. As each of them works in the medicine wheel, they learn the lessons of Forgiveness.

It's important that we start in the spirit—the East gate. We are in the spirit because, though we live in the physical realm, we are always in a medicine wheel. As we walk into the medicine wheel in a symbolic way, we always start in the East and walk clockwise. Each time we cross a stone, we understand something more. It's interesting to go up the line of lessons— the cross in the middle of the wheel—because you're standing in a gate, and you always walk forward to do the lessons. As you complete one line of lessons, walking around the burgundy lesson clockwise, you come back through the same lessons. So, walking the lessons is what the students have learned, and we walk past the same lesson over and over and over in life.

Those are my final words tonight about lessons, for next week it is the Will we will look at, and inner peace that we will be talking about.

I watch their eyes twinkle when I tell them the value of understanding, of knowing the lessons. There is nothing more vital to life than understanding the spiritual, living with the emotions, and being intact in our physicality. Our whole purpose in being human is to be intact, to feel the wholeness, and to understand the lessons. I think it's funny how everyone always wants to know where he or she comes from—always wanting to detach, always wanting to divide.

"That's what humans do," I hear her say.

I breathe in and out and look the old one in the face. She is thin and very, very old. Her eyes are yellow, deep and sunken. She has strong features in her wrinkled face. Her hair is snow white and pulled back. She has on a baseball cap backwards. She is wearing a blouse, blue jeans, and beautifully beaded moccasins. She can't be very tall, but she isn't stout in her smallness.

I look closely and I can see the wolf. I see it in the intensity of her eyes.

"Oh, but you're wrong, Wolf. I'm not a wolf. I'm a trout speaking—a fish. We are close to the wolf, for we're aloof, but if you follow us, you'll find the secrets of forgiveness. If you look at our life, you'll see that we're simple. When something snags us or holds onto us, we just let go. We return to the same spot and nestle in, and live one breath at a time. It is mine to share with you forgiveness. It's time for you, as you're walking the river, to come to that place where the ice is no more, where you have crossed the depth of winter and are standing very close to the spring. It is a day when the snow falls heavy in the sky, but settles lightly on the ground."

I look into her eyes and feel very comfortable. I feel I can trust her.

She sits on a rock looking at the river and points, "He's right over there.

Right there is a hatch. That's the place where he lives, you know—the trout—the one who is the story of the rainbow."

"Why does he have spots?" I ask.

She looks at me and says, "Oh, the stories in his life. Is that what you want to know? Well, he is the keeper of Knowledge, and the bigger he is, the more spots he has, and the more times he's won a battle. He knows the story of the dark nights."

I look in her eyes and see everything. I see tomorrow and all it holds. Her eyes show me the path I follow and want all students to know. We sit there by the river in the pines and listen to the birds sing their song. We listen to the elks clashing their horns against the trees and walking through the woods. I smell early Spring.

"Don't rush it, Wolf. You're still in the North. It's not Spring yet. You're not standing in the fullness of spirit. You still have to understand the dots, the black spots. You see, the trout is a soul. It is the best example of the soul that there is on the Earth, for it is an existing rainbow, and each spot is a story of a dark night. The dark night is where the soul has been saddened or put to sleep. In essence, though, it's a loss of energy," she says with intensity. "It's important to have the soul intact, for it is your path and the soul is made of complete energy, and complete energy is Knowledge. Grandmother/Grandfather/Great Spirit/Creator sends you out in Knowledge, gives you memory, and knowing. You might say a soul is a path of Knowledge."

"Hmm," I say and scratch behind my ear. "I've always thought your soul is who you are, the very inner self."

"No, no, dear, you are the walk of your soul. In your life walk, you are the teacher. You bring Color to the people. You give medicine to those who seek. The soul is the path of Truth and Confidence. It is the connection to Great Spirit. When humankind has Knowledge and understands inner peace, they are connected to the soul."

I feel a soft cool breeze blow as she speaks.

"In the spirit world the river is the flow. You come to the North for you are from the North. The brain/mind and soul are the way of the river. Ice, snow, rains—all flow—they are of the river. Water is the way to see Great Spirit clearly. The North opens the doorway to the soul and the Understanding of the self. You, Wolf, are like all humankind. You are looking for the way home, and home is the wholeness of the self. The Vision you have has brought you to your center, to the Will of Great Spirit. At the river you found the self and came to understand love from Dark Eyes. You see, whether you call him father, grandfather, brother, or lover, it is all the same—the male. In the spirit it is known as the strong one. the provider or the Strength. On the earth, because of life, it is known as the male. The woman is sister, mother, grandmother, friend, lover, or wife. A male and female are Energy. Like the river, they are flow. Because they can think and have emotions, they can make life very complex, when actually, as the river, the flow is easy. The voice of the river speaks to all, as you do—it teaches. As the students come to the river they learn."

I look at her and say, "I come from the river."

She laughs a sweet laugh and says, "You are of the River People. The flow of life, the continual movement of the soul."

"Is it true that each person has a soul, or is a bunch of beings connected to a soul?"

"No, no, each has a soul. That makes up the swirling mass of Color. As you go to Grandfather/Grandmother/Creator/God, you'll see a massive amount of Color—that is the souls intermingling, intertwining, making the connections that make everything happen."

"So, the soul is Knowledge?" I ask.

"The soul is pure Energy and pure Energy is knowing, we open to our soul from knowing. As we know our spirit self through the thoughts of the mind, we have guidance from our soul. The flow of life is the Energy of everything coming together, as in the river. Just think of the soul as the river," she says.

She crosses her arms, leans back on the rock and looks into the sky. "The trout knows. The trout knows the rainbow, the soul, the pathway home. The Trout knows that the darkness is only humankind's fears. The darkness is sadness, it's sickness, it's unforgiving. It's where I can't see myself anymore. It's what brings about the dark nights, the tears, the emptiness in the soul. But the darkness is just the bottom of the river. The trout sees in the dark, therefore, it sees through the darkness, and it is a chance to learn. To seek and find."

She breathes in and out gently, and I notice that she is real pale. She's hardly even before my eyes, she's so faint, and the faintness is a beautiful silver, purplish color.

"Why are you so pale?"

She looks at me. "You are in the Spirit World. The paler it is the more powerful it is, you understand?"

"So on Earth is it important to be bold and powerful?"

"As you are bold and powerful," she nods. "Yes. You are strong in your medicine. You remember and you know and everything is clear to you."

I watch the river passing by and I see a large trout jumping, the colors on his side glistening in the sunlight. "Tell me more about the soul," I say.

It is quiet. I turn around to look at her, and she is gone. As I watch the ocean, a pathway appears on the water shimmering, inviting me to follow.

"It's time, it's time for you to go out there, Wolf." It is a voice I don't recognize.

An old man is standing before me. He's strongly built with a big belly. He looks like he's German or Irish. He has beautiful blue eyes, a long, white beard, and his heavy white hair lies in waves on his shoulders. He is wearing an old worn out hat, a cowboy hat, and he's holding the reins to a mule.

I ask him, "Who might you be?"

"Oh, you can call me Donkey Man." I look closely and his eyes shine. He smiles and his right tooth is a star—a purple star with a diamond in the center. His hands are withered and old but thick and powerful.

He points to the ocean. "I think that's where you're going. I think out there is that doorway you're looking for. But you must know that she was right about forgiveness. You can't walk into that doorway and go into spirit to the face of the Creator and have anger in your heart. Is there anything that you need to let go of?"

As he says that, the old mule gives out a neigh and sucks in and out. I always love to hear the hee-haw of a mule.

The old man puts his hand on the mule's ears and shakes its head.

"Yes, he's mine. He's my best friend. This is Beaker. He's been with me for 18 years. I think it's a good thing to walk with your stubbornness. I think it's a good thing to understand that all humans are stubborn. There are only two kinds of humans, Wolf; that's a mean human or a stubborn human. The mule is forgiveness medicine. It's important to understand the teachings of the trout, for that is Knowledge medicine. You know that the soul is a sacred part of your existence, and out there goes your soul—out there through the water, to the place you've been told about, and then beyond, into the Understanding of Will, and to inner peace. You will be in the face of Great Spirit."

"Why is it," I ask, "that we're separated in the spirit world?"

He looks at me quickly and says, "We're not separated. This is all one place, one doorway to the next, one doorway to the next. That's how it works here."

"It looks like it's hidden," I say. "It's different in the physical realm."

"Yeah, well," he says, "it isn't hidden, you just gotta know. You've come to the depth of Knowledge. Your truths have brought principles into your

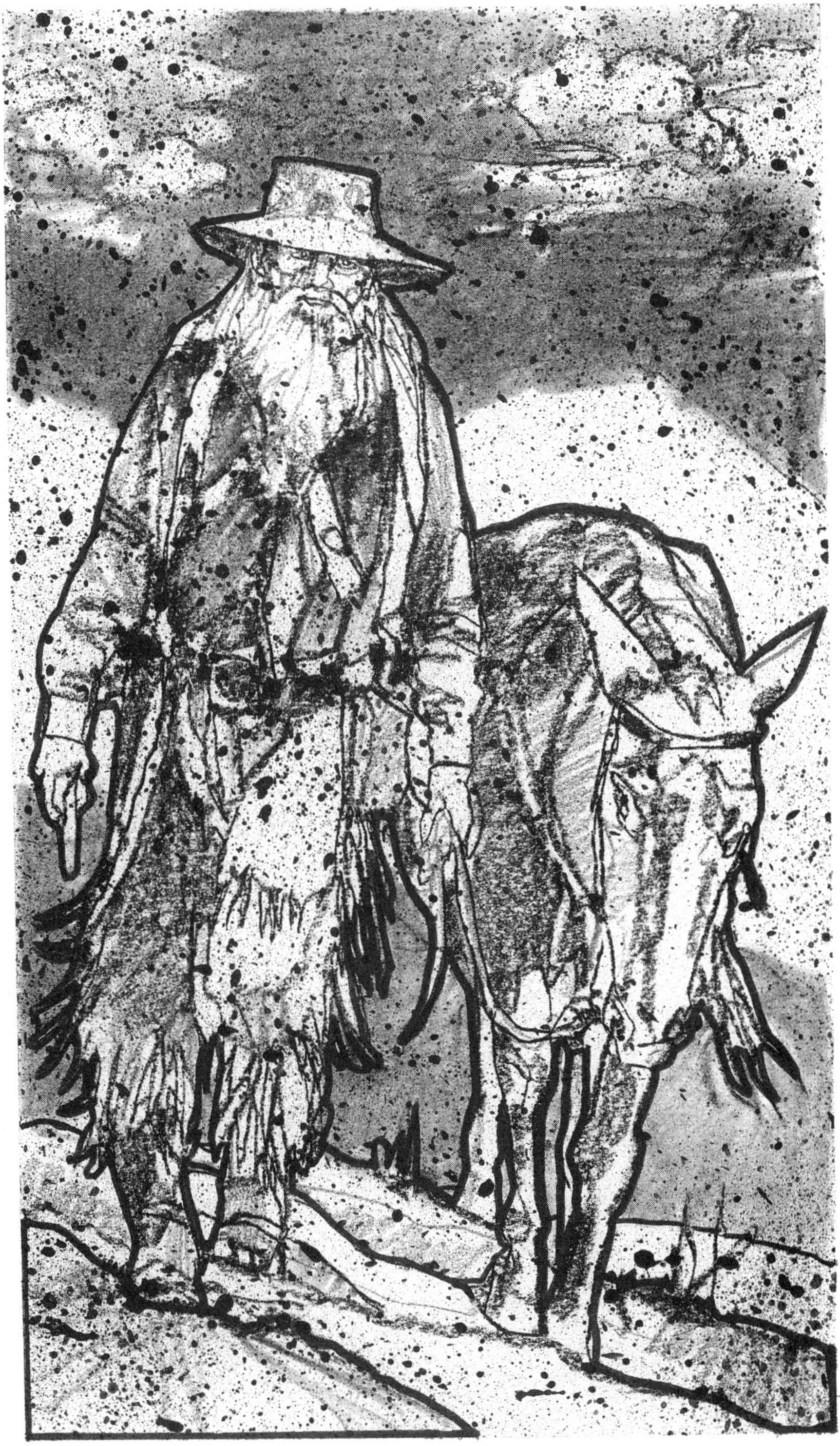

existence that make you aware. You have the insight to be well informed and make clear decisions. Yes, I see." He strokes his white beard and spits some chewing tobacco on the ground. "I see this."

I look at him and at the chewing tobacco and say, "Chewing tobacco in the spirit world?"

"Well, you know stranger things do happen."

I stare at him for a minute. "There is a reason for this, isn't there?"

"Yep!" He says, nodding his head. He pushes his old hat back, and looks me right straight in the eye.

I know that he is looking for me to judge him. "Ah, I don't have any judgment towards you. It's none of my business. That way, you say? Head out that way—just walk out into the water and keep going?"

He says, "I'll imagine you'll figure it out pretty soon." He puts his hand on my shoulder. "It won't be long before they call you a wise old wolf." He pats me on the back and is gone in the twink of an eye.

"I sure love how people come and go in this place," I laugh.

Well, I take the bundle and I start walking and in front of me I come upon a pool of water. It's a pretty good sized pool, and as I look at it, I see wavy lines around it. The pool is etched in a rainbow and its colors weave up and down, making it a waving rainbow. I walk into the pool and stand in the colors. I look down in the water, at my reflection. I am old, very old. My face is weathered and wrinkled, and my teeth are gone. I move my mouth and my chin touches my nose. I can see my mom. I see her eyes—those deep-set, beady eyes—looking back at me.

I close my eyes, take a breath, and look again. Now a beautiful white wolf is staring back at me. I become one with the wolf. I feel the mist of the water as I ride on the wolf's back. I feel the wolf's feet take to the air, but it is only me in flight. My paws touch the path of glistening light. Thousands and thousands of stars glisten beneath my feet. I leave the mist and begin to rise.

**I hear the howl of the wolf calling me back.**

# THE TEACHINGS OF KNOWLEDGE—TROUT MEDICINE

The medicine of Knowledge is the Wisdom humankind walks with. To have Knowledge you need Respect, knowing, and Nurture. Knowledge is an on-going study. As a humankind, you never stop learning, so the movement of Knowledge is continual. When you have Knowledge in your life you can hear the voice of your soul as well as all the connecting souls.

The soul is your sacred path, which is a part of the Good Red Road, the spiritual path of Great Spirit. With each lesson we learn comes a knowing that builds our Knowledge. Knowledge is our dreams and goals and Vision. We can have no Success without Knowledge. As you go to learn the lessons of life, remember that Ceremony is Knowledge, Vision is Knowledge, Prayer is Knowledge, shamanic journey is Knowledge, memory is Knowledge, all is Knowledge.

As a humankind it is easy to be in denial, which is a mental illness, a part of depression, and depression is a chemical imbalance in the brain. When you overlook or turn a deaf ear to these matters in your life, it can be serious; you can be within the grasp of death. Applying Knowledge means looking around and watching others and what happens to them—knowing what you want for yourself and obtaining it.

Knowledge is seen in the trout, the spirit totem. The trout stays close to where it was born. It might swim away to eat or mate, but it always returns to its birthplace to die, for the Knowledge of home stays in its memory.

Knowledge is soul knowing. We are all spirit and in that Knowledge we are all able to know the importance of happiness and joy. In soul knowing you have the ability to take actions that teach you and bring forth habits. The soul is the place from which you draw pure spiritual energy. This energy activates the neurological patterns in your brain, which are the thoughts of your mind.

Knowledge is habits. As humankind learns, it remembers and memory is Knowledge.

Aho!

## CEREMONY OF THE INNER WOLF

**Tools::** *Strips of cloth cut 36 inches (90cm) long by 2 inches (5cm) wide—one silver, one blue, one white, and one burgundy; sticks on which to tie the* *strips of cloth — they need to be 6 feet (1.8m) tall — or you can tie the strips onto a tree; journal and pen; smudging supplies.*

The Ceremony of the Inner Wolf is done to bring forth your inner teacher, to bring forth your ability to guide and teach yourself. During this Ceremony you may also be directed to someone else who will guide or direct you.

There are four phases of the inner wolf:

The baby wolf — this is your hopes and your dreams, the things you enjoy, the places you like the most. You might like sitting among the trees, for example, because you liked to climb them when you were young. You might like to go for picnics and walk along the river or pond, because this was where you went when you were a child. The places you like mostly date back to your younger days.

The young wolf — this wolf is young to life, lanky and full of zest. It directs you to your Vision, and your Vision is your road map to life.

The adult wolf — the mature wolf understands the value of what you do in life. This wolf reminds you that you must survive, so it talks about discipline and obedience, and ways to be successful.

The elder wolf — this wolf shows you what you have gained from your life; that the lessons of life have given you certain abilities. The elder wolf reveals your Creativity, and sets forth an image of you as a parent, grandparent, great grandparent, that young ones can speak of and draw Strength from. It shows that your walk in life reflects Wisdom, Knowledge, intellect, and intelligence.

These four wolves are involved with teaching you how to know your path in life. The wolf is the pathfinder in the spirit realm. It will show you how to understand life. The wolf is the guide for the mental realm. You will want to list the following questions and answer them.

1. What is your mind?
2. How do you use your mind?
3. What allows you to have a mind on your two-legged walk?
4. What do you need to do to have a healthy mind?

Answer these questions and apply them as an Understanding from your wolf guide. After you have answered them, tie the white cloth to one of the sticks, smudge it, and move on to the next set of questions.

Answer the next questions about the brain, understanding that your brain is similar to a parent, and as the brain matures, the mind evolves, and thinking is the action of life. The brain is the home of the mind. The brain is physical and the mind is spiritual.

1. What is your brain?
2. How do you use your brain?
3. What allows you to have a brain on your two-legged walk?
4. What do you need to do to have a healthy brain?

As you answer these questions, reflect on the brain as your parent. Think of yourself being raised by your brain as you answer them. Also, take your time answering these questions, so that you can come to understand your brain. Consult a psychiatrist or neurologist, or a specialist that studies the brain, or go on the Internet and get information there that will give you an understanding of your brain, the synapse process, the neurological process in your brain, and what it does for you.

When you have answered the parent part of the Ceremony, tie the blue flag onto the pole, smudge it and move on to the next set of questions.

This group of questions is the pathfinder part of your inner wolf, your soul. Answer these questions:

1. What is your soul? How do you know that?
2. How do you use your soul?
3. What allows you to have a soul on your two-legged walk?
4. What do you need to do to have a healthy soul?

It is very important that you have a clear understanding of your soul.

Remember, I teach that the soul is not spirit, but the pathway that spirit walks on. It is the connection that is never broken between you and Grandmother/Grandfather/Great Spirit and the land of spirit, as you walk through the lessons of life.

As a human, you can walk out to the edge of your soul, or you can walk to the sides of your soul, but you can never turn around and walk back on your soul into the spirit world—unless you travel there in shamanic journey, or unless you drop your robe (die as a human being).

When you have answered the pathfinder part of the Ceremony, tie the silver flag to a stick, smudge it, and move on to the next set of questions.

The fourth section, the teacher part of the inner wolf, deals with your beliefs. Answer the following questions:

1. What is your teacher?
2. How do you use your teacher?
3. What allows you to have a teacher on your two-legged walk?
4. What do you need to do to have a healthy teacher?

Anything, everything, and all that teaches you, qualifies you as a teacher. Put the emphasis on what teaches you the most. What is teaching you today? What has taught you in previous years, and why do you have to be taught?

When you have answered the teacher part of this Ceremony, take the burgundy flag, tie it to the stick, and smudge it.

The reason that you tie the flags onto the sticks or onto a tree is to celebrate your understanding of your inner wolf. Dig a hole and place the sticks in the ground so that the flags can fly freely. Let the flags stay and blow in the breeze that represents the Balance, the Knowledge, the Understanding, and the Wisdom of the mental plane.

If you have no yard and no place to tie the flags, then you need to find someone who will allow you to place them on their property. Or find sacred ground on which you can place your flags, such as a forest, a state park, or someplace else where your flags will be welcomed as a belief.

As you place these flags, you will understand your inner wolf. You will understand the four directions of the wolf from the baby, the young, the mature, and the elder wolf, to the guide, the parent, the pathfinder, and the teacher. These movements of your inner wolf are important for your mind and brain, as well as for your soul and spirit voice to be in Balance.

Any time you feel you are separating from the Knowledge of your ability to be balanced in the mental section of the Rainbow Medicine Wheel, it is a good thing to do the Ceremony of the Inner Wolf. If you perform the Ceremony again, it's okay to tie the strips onto the same sticks, and it's okay to place new sticks, if you want.

Having visual contact with the flags on the sticks or on the tree reminds you daily that you need to accept the limits of the brain and perceive the mind as the voice of spirit. It's important that you, as a human two-legged, understand that the spirit guides us. We are limited in our memory, but we can expand that memory when we open to the realms of spirit to allow them to speak to us. As we expand those realms, the teacher part of our inner wolf speaks to us in our beliefs.

# THE BASKET OF KNOWLEDGE STONES

**Tools:** *A woven basket with a handle; rocks; as many as you'll need to represent the answers to your questions; a white candle; paint that is not water soluble in the colors of red, white, blue, and silver; 7 colors of ribbon, 1/4 inch (6mm) wide, in red, orange, yellow, green, blue, purple, and burgundy; your journal and pen; smudge tools.*

This basket holds stones with symbols on them that are connected with your personal life and study. It will help you Understand your deeper self and the four sections of your self. Each rock in the basket is a stone of Knowledge.

You perform the Ceremony on a full moon day in the high noon sunlight. You sit with the stones and have gratitude for the Knowledge you have in your life. Take each stone, hold it, and listen to your thoughts, to your inner guides, to your questions about life, to the voice of spirit coming through your mind. Then you write in your journal about what you feel, hear, or see while touching the Knowledge stones.

Start by weaving the seven colored ribbons through the handle of the basket. If you can not weave the ribbons through the handle, then wrap them around it so that the handle looks like a rainbow. Tie them where the handle connects to the basket, and allow some of the ribbon to hang off both sides. (You may weave the ribbons through your basket, too, if you want to give the basket color, or tie pieces of ribbon to the basket in any way you want.)

143

The basket is a safe place in which to keep your Knowledge stones. You put Knowledge stone in your basket every time you have earned one, which is any time you feel that you have come to a full understanding of something in your life. An earned Knowledge is a knowing. When you have this knowing, take a stone and decide if the knowing is from the mind, or from a physical action that belongs to the brain, or a pathway action that belongs to the soul, or a spiritual knowing that has come to you, which links it to the spirit. The mind is represented by red; the soul or spiritual path is represented by silver; the brain, by blue; and the spiritual knowing by white.

The following questions will help you obtain Knowledge stones. Answer them in your journal..

## SPIRITUAL KNOWING

**1. How do you see spirit?** Define your ability to see spirit. Do you feel it's a knowing? Do you actually see a picture like a movie in your thoughts? Do you see one image that is a Vision? Elaborate on your spiritual knowing.

**2. Do you hear spirit talk to you? If so, what does the voice sound like? Whose voice is it?** What do you think of when you hear this voice of spirit?

**3. When you have a spiritual knowing, does it come from something someone said to you?** Something you saw on TV? Something that you feel deep down inside of you, that you call your heart? Define and give examples to yourself of what your spiritual knowing is.

**4. Why do you think that, as a human two-legged, you need a connection to spiritual knowing?** Give examples of why you have spiritual knowing.

> **Example:** *To guide you through dark nights, to help you in time of sickness, to give you Courage and Strength to carry on in times of weakness or situations such as divorce, family turmoil, and death..*

You may also place a stone in your basket for your animal guide, for your inner guide ("the small voice within"), for your personal guide (a guide you have trusted for a long time), for your guardians (ways and thoughts and feelings that you know you can trust, that never let you down).

# THE SOUL—PATHWAY OF THE SPIRIT

**1. What is your soul to you?** In your journal write about what you think your soul is. Where did you learn about your soul? Who was the one who taught you about your soul?

Find a stone that represents your soul and place it in the basket. You can have more than one stone.

**2. Can you see your soul as a pathway?**
A soul is a silver-blue connection of energy that connects you and the Great Spirit. It allows you to forgive and be forgiven. It allows the Energy from Great Spirit to guide and direct you. It is your connection is with your spirit guides and the spirit world. Find a silver-blue stone to represent the Energy of the soul pathway and place it in your basket.

**3. What does your soul look like? Have you ever been able to see your soul and understand the connection between Great Spirit and the physical plane?** When you take a spirit journey you can look at the soul connection. Knowing your soul connection is the action of believing. The soul is a silver cord or a path of silver-blue light. It connects you to your physical body and to Great Spirit. Describe the soul as you see it in your journal.

> **Example** (*a student's soul description*): *I saw a very shiny cord that connected me to a wonderful bright white light. I could follow the cord to the bright light. I know it was my soul.*

Write in your journal words that help explain your soul connection.

> **Example:** *Soft, bright, wide, loud, strong.*

Find rocks for the words that explain your soul connection and place them in your basket.

**4. What do you need to do to have a healthy soul?**
This is the action that keeps you connected to your soul. These are actions of Choice. List the actions you will take to keep the soul healthy. List them in your journal.

> **Example:** *A walk in nature. Listening to music that feeds the soul, happy, clear tones and tunes. Spiritual actions—Prayer and Ceremony that is connected to the light. Sharing things with people, working with dreams and Visions, reading and studying Truth and Knowledge.*

# THE BRAIN

Brain Knowledge is physical knowing, in areas such as family, sexuality, wellness, illnesses, directions to take, automatic thinking processes.

**1. Why is your brain important to your physical existence?**

**2. Can you exist without your brain?**
   a. Explain how, if you can.
   b. What would be the quality of life without the brain?
   c. What kills a brain?
   d. How would your body function without a brain? What would keep the body alive if you did not have a brain? Would you be placed on life support and keep your body alive without any thought actions, speech, writing or any self-expression?

**3. List the mental actions of humankind.** These are physical actions: eating, sexual activity, reproduction. They would include having a job, owning a home, owning all the stuff you have—boat, car, yard, things. List these as actions, choose a stone, and place it in the basket.

**4. Choose from the following brain actions the things you like or don't like about humankind.** Sickness, chemical problems: drug use, drinking problems, mental afflictions, sexual problems, interaction problems, weight problems, reading problems, criminal problems, lying problems, Place a stone in the basket for your humankind problems.

# THE MIND

**1. List in your journal, the areas of your mind you know and understand.**

   *Example: Thought, details, feelings, emotions, daydreams, nightmares, spiritual knowing, connections with your Vision or dreams. This is where your connection is with your higher self, and your relationship to the spirit world, heaven, or whatever name you call the place you go after physical life. Gather a stone for each Understanding you have and place in the basket.*

**2. Gather a stone for actions of the mind that you do in your daily life:** Sing, write, draw, hobbies, spend time with friends and loved ones, set goals.

**3. Gather a stone for each of the following concepts you believe in:**

Write the Understanding you have for each one of them in your journal. These are Understandings that are guided by the mind.

1. Life
2. Death
3. Spirits
4. Healing
5. Knowledge
6. Life after death
7. Your spiritual home.

Place a stone in the basket for each guide that helps you in the spirit world.

Every answer that you give is a knowing. Choose a rock that corresponds to the knowing and paint a symbol on it in the appropriate color. Select symbols from the area the Knowledge stone deals with: mind, brain, soul, spirit. When you add a stone, listen to the knowing and it will tell you where it goes.

Any time that you realize that you have a knowing, it's a good idea to grab a rock, and prepare it. Cleanse it by lighting your sage and letting it smolder and smoke. Pass the stone through the smoke four times to balance the Energy, then wash it with clean water, and dry it. Take a journey to find your symbol that goes on the stone. Look for a symbol that represents your connection to the stone. Draw it in pictograph style, which is simple—it can be just stick figures, elementary art. Make the symbol easy to read so you can remember its meaning.

After you have painted the stones, place them in the basket and use them in your Knowledge Stone Ceremony, or simply set the basket at your altar and celebrate the amount of Knowledge you have. Keep the basket at your altar when you are not using it.

When you choose, go to the basket, open your journal, and work with thoughts about the stones. Journal how you use the actions connected with each stone. When you have learned the lesson of the stone, remove it and place it in a pile at your medicine wheel or at your altar.

You may add new stones to the basket at any time. These stones are your personal connection to your deeper self.

Aho.

# THE LESSON OF FORGIVENESS—THE MULE

Forgiveness is the need to settle your fears and move on to acceptance. As you forgive you dismiss the pain and hurt. You may never forget, if you choose, but you must dismiss the pain and hurt. When this happens, forgiveness can take place.

When you are hurt, the first person you need to forgive is yourself. You are the one in control of your Choices. You are in control of your pain. When you are learning the lesson of forgiveness, you need to reflect on the actions of others and see how you let yourself be hurt.

The lesson within forgiveness is to see the Strength in yourself. You will need to apply the Understanding of the totem of the mule. The mule is steadfast and sure, slow and simple. To gain Knowledge from the lesson of forgiveness, you need to admit to the yourself that you might look like the mule, and people may confuse your steadfastness for stubbornness. The mule is determined. When you forgive, you must be like the mule.

To learn the lesson of forgiveness, you need to walk away from and let go of. You need to totally dismiss the past to truly forgive. You do not harbor grudges or bring harm to another. You do not wish to get even or see the need to settle a score. To forgive is not turning a cheek. Bring reason to your emotions. Forgiveness is dismissal. It happens when you Balance your emotions and accept things as they are. When you get hurt look at the lesson. Find the teaching within why you have pain and make choices that bring about change. Forgiveness is showing your joy and ability to forget and move on. When you learn the lesson of forgiveness, you have learned to see all things as a lesson and apply medicine to your life from the colors.

As you walk in the Rainbow Medicine Wheel, it is all of life. It shows that you and all are one circle, equal and balanced. The Energy brings about Strength in the soul. We can and do live a life that shows our true Colors.

Aho!

# NOTE FROM WOLF MOONDANCE

Human beings mimic each other. It's easy to understand that the brain is mechanical. It goes through its functions and creates its avenues. Stress also creates avenues, habits create avenues, and lack of habits creates avenues. Behaviors are avenues. So are patterns of thinking, memories, and the suggestions of others. As we want to live with our spiritual thoughts, we must understand the conditions in the brain.

I recommend that you study the neurology of the brain. Anyone, no matter what the limitations of thinking are—even those who have been made to feel inadequate in intelligence—can open up this realm of Understanding by looking into the area of neurology.

I believe that a daily Prayer life is imperative. Also, it's important that you have the privilege to think as you wish, for your beliefs are based on your experiences and opinions. Think about the human brain as a recorder. It records everybody's teachings, everybody's suggestions, everybody's demands, and commands.

The brain is also greatly affected by the amount of rest you get, what your eating habits are, what your drug habits are, what your habits in general are, and what chemicals you put into your body that affect the synapse process.

We all may not understand words like schizophrenic, or psychotic, or depression, or chronic personality disorders such as Borderline Personality Disorder that goes with Bipolar Depression. But it's important that we understand that those terms are beliefs about the synapse process within the physical brain. And all diseases, including cancer, AIDS, and severe mental psychological problems, have to do with chemical imbalances in the brain.

Also, sugar—any form of sugar—nicotine, alcohol, hallucinogenic drugs, and every other type of drug affects the chemical balance of the brain. Researchers are looking for answers to the entire chemical imbalance question, and they've come a long way since the 1800's when discipline was basically the answer to just about every problem.

There always has been imbalanced mental behavior that causes dark nights, which are black spots in the soul. I like to think of them as the chug holes in the road. When our soul becomes weakened, it weakens the force of our chakras, the main Energy points in the body.

Please understand that everything in life is a belief, and those beliefs are a part of our soul, which is the path we walk as individuals.

The mind is spirit, and the brain provides a home for the spirit while the spirit is learning lessons, which is what the human existence is all about. If the brain is damaged or in poor condition, the spirit can be rejected. What happens to a rejected spirit? That lies in the realms of mystery. It might be what ghosts are. Without the brain, the thoughts of the mind are spirit. The brain is physical matter.

You know, as we walk in the medicine wheel, we can all give our opinions, and we can all assume things. We can all fantasize, speak, and blow hot air. An infinite number of souls come together to produce the Rainbow Path. It takes a tremendous amount of energy to bring forth the perpetual motion of existence. Take your chances, go ahead, deal the hand, and then ask yourself how it's going to play out. Knowledge lies in Understanding the teacher, the voice of the inner wolf.

Aho.

# 10 ◆ THE WATERFALL OF JOY—HOME

I breathe in and out and I relax. The seven students have finished. They are given the option of going on to the center and listening to Sweet Medicine. They all make their commitments. They shake hands with me and leave for vacation, giving themselves time to organize and prepare for the study that lies ahead.

As I gather my medicine tools and bundle them up, I look at the candles before me and feel my mind quiet down. I see an opening in the ocean. I know this is where I am to go. I draw on the energy of my soul and walk through the opening. I enter into the deepest part of spirit. It is very quiet; the burgundy color is so intense it is black.

The sky glitters with sparks of light. Before me, I see lightning bugs, thousands and thousands of lightning bugs. One minute they are lightning bugs, the next minute they are glistening stars. I see the path that guides me into the teachings of

Will. I follow this path. It is dirt, black dirt. I smell its fresh aroma.

As I walk, I pass by trees, an orchard. The trees smell wonderful. Their blooms have come and their fragrance is powerful.

I see a spirit dressed in black and white—its shirt white, pants black. Its boots are black with white fur. The spirit is neither male nor female. Its form is similar to a human, but it is a spirit. Its face is black on one side and white on the other. On the black side, its hair is long and white. On the white side, its hair is short and black. Its eyes are painted with a large black star with six smaller stars cascading down to its chin. It has an earring made of one perfect bubble that is all seven colors.

The spirit changes to a magpie, sits on the ground in front of me, and then flies northeast. Lightning bugs glisten in the trees and I hear the roar of a waterfall. I stop and look out across a peaceful valley, as a voice speaks these words, "Determination, Wolf. Be sure, Wolf, you have the ability. You must take deliberate action. You are in the Power of choosing where your desire is no longer a wish but a reality. You have purpose. You must know your purpose."

I turn and before me are seven lines of the different colors—red, orange, yellow, green, blue, purple, and burgundy. "Cross the lines. These lines are the Will of Great Spirit/Grandmother/Grandfather."

I cross the first line and I hear the word "Ability."

As I walk across the line, I see a time in my childhood when my life almost ended, and I see me making it. I remember the first time I drew with my mother and painted a picture. She said, "You have the ability, girl."

I see the orange line, and I hear the word "Determination." I remember times where my sureness carried me to the next movement. I see a medicine wheel and I know that I am sure. I step across the orange line.

I step across the yellow line and I hear, "Deliberate action." I stand there and see all my teachers. I see the gifts of giving. I see the pain of a martyr and I know that life is given for opportunity. It is a knowing that I have. I look down and I am walking my path. The knowing is of my soul.

I step across the green line and hear, "Power of choosing." As I step across the line, I am shown many Choices in my life, when to quit, when to go on, what to do, what not to do.

I see the blue line and hear, "Desire, your wish." I look in the sky and see colored bubbles cascading down and bouncing on the ground. I step on through the bubbles.

I cross the purple line and hear the word "Fun." I hear laughter.

I see the burgundy line and I hear the word "Purpose." As I step across the purpose line, I hear nothing. I see nothing. Everything is white.

A soft gentle voice speaks. "We will take you to a place where you will see, where you will be in the presence of what two-leggeds would call 'the face of the Creator.' We would like you to know that to obtain inner peace, you must believe that you can see, and that is the face. You must face all things. There is a secret within all Knowledge. When you are told that you cannot see the face, you are in the face. When you are told you're not good enough to be a part of, you should walk away from. Much of the mental illness, the sickness, and the unhappiness comes from a lack—a lack of facing the truth. When you are small, you can be lied to and your whole life will be out of balance. You have lived with the truth and you face the face."

I hear the wind blowing through the pines, the sounds of the ocean, the rushing river. The sounds become loud. I smell the woods, the river flock, a flower that grows by the river, and home cooking. I hear children laughing.

Before me is an enormous waterfall and there in front of me are these small light beings—little spirits with wings that are similar to fairies. They are all colors, bold and pastel. They hover above the water at the base of the waterfall. One of them runs up to me. Its little face is round, pudgy. Its body is also round and soft like a bubble. Its wings are transparent. Its color is shades of orange and it shimmers with gold.

"Join us, Wolf! Come take a ride in the waterfall. Feel the feeling of inner peace. Join us!"

I hear laughter, and hundreds and hundreds of lights surround me.

I find myself in a bubble with several light beings, rising in the air. I feel free and light. We bounce on the top of the waterfall and float, rolling head over heels, tumbling down. I see the bubbles bursting as they hit the water and shoot in all directions. Everything is color.

I rise again in another bubble and bounce on the waterfall. Laughter and joy fills my heart. I find myself in the water. It is warm and comfortable, and many light spirits are washing, dancing, and singing in the water with me. They swirl around and around. I feel the colors all around me, and float on the river of color. The river winds and turns as I float gently along.

I stop. I feel a hand on my shoulder. It is the Blue-Eyed Raven. He pulls me out of the water, spins me around, and I dry in the air. Standing behind me, he puts his arms around me.

"Look ahead of you, Wolf."

I look and there is the most beautiful sight I have ever seen—a glorious area with many trees and ferns. The mist of the water rises above the waterfall and sparkles with reds, blues, oranges, purples, greens, yellows, and burgundies. The ground is covered with soft ferns and clover—four-leaf clovers are all around me. The air is soft and filled with the gentle scent of flowers.

"Your soul is connected to this place," he says. "This is home."

I hear the laughter of children, many children, and hear the sounds of animals, the purring, the growling, the clicking and singing of the birds.

"Wolf, look up."

I look up through the mist of the waterfall, and see two faces with smiles and blue eyes. The faces are neither male nor female, though they are similar to humans—they have eyes, noses, and mouths, and curly cascading hair. One is silver and one is gold. They are two together in the clouds above the waterfall. There is a full moon and to the sides of it are radiant crescent moons with brilliant silver, purple, and blue light shooting out on the left and the right.

The light reaches out, and as it does, it rainbows. Each crescent moon's light splits into rainbow colors and the bands shoot outward. In between each crescent moon are seven colored stars that sparkle and shoot lights back into the faces of the spirits.

"This is the Will of Great Spirit—home," the Blue-Eyed Raven says.

A magpie lands in the tree in front of me. I see lightning bugs sparkling around the waterfall.

"It is nothing but light," I say.

"Do you wish that it that it was more?"

Suddenly, as I look at the waterfall, it becomes a light being with wings. Its gown is the cascading waterfall, and a lovely, soft, pale burgundy face is at the top of the being. Each tree has a face and now is a being. Everything is alive with light and color reflected in the waterfall.

"This is the Will of Great Spirit," I say.

"Yes Wolf, it is light. Where there is light, there is the Will of Great

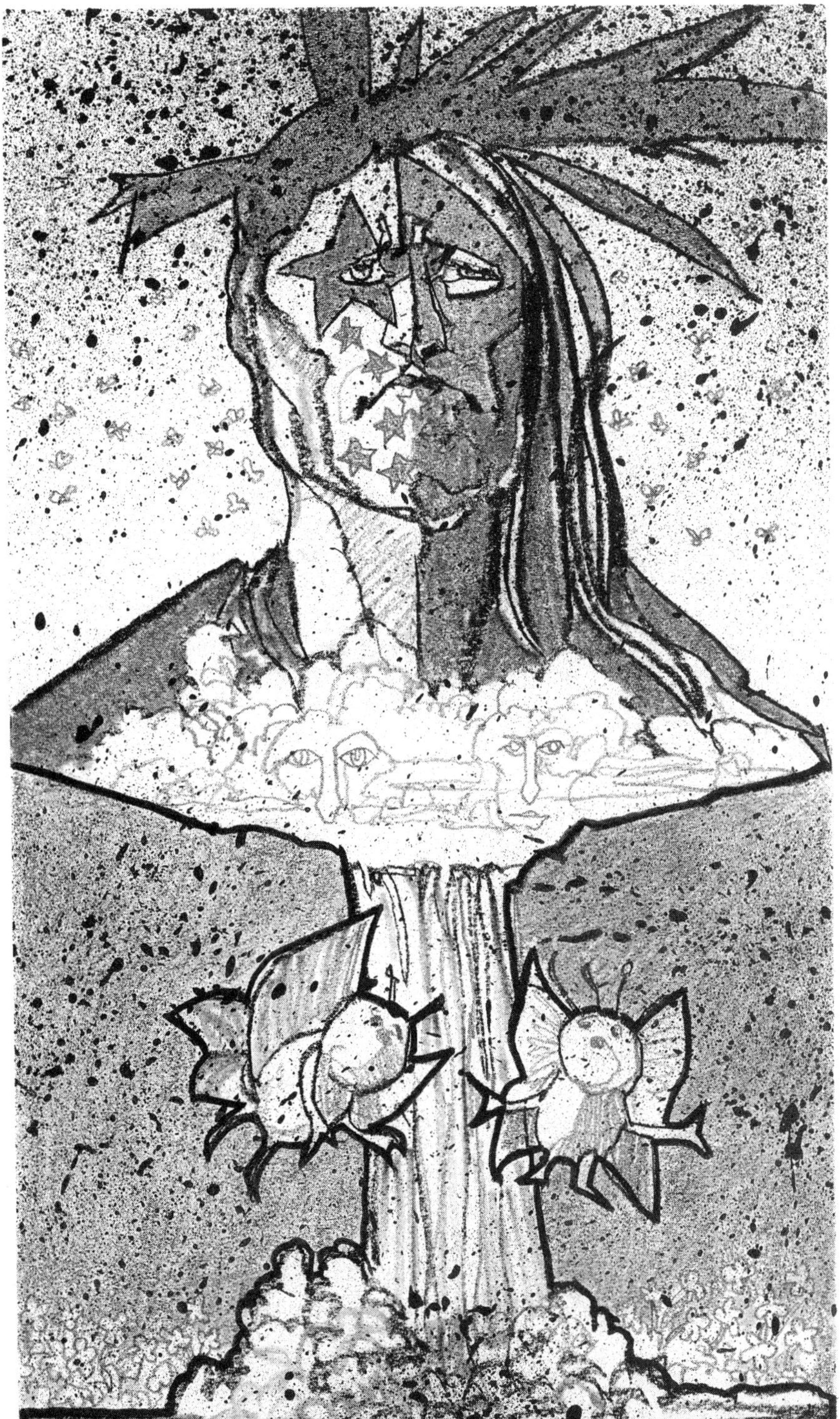

Spirit, and the song of the wolf and the story of the coyote, and the magic of the raven, and the spirit of the eagle, and the Prayer of the buffalo, and the splendor of the mountains, and the solitude of the ocean. It is the Will of Great Spirit."

I feel his love embrace me. I take a deep breath in and out.

"I could breathe this light forever, Raven."

"You will, Wolf," he says. "It is the Will of Great Spirit that we teach the joy of the Good Red Road. It is here where all races change to colors and all Color is the same."

The mist blows in my face. I have walked the Rainbow Path, and now I realize that it is my soul. It is the eternal infinite connection between Great Spirit and me.

"I have seen the face, Raven."

"Yes, Wolf. You are home."

I feel soft gentle hands on my shoulders. I turn and see Grandmother and Grandfather Wolf. The four of us embrace.

"I knew you'd find your way here," Grandfather says. "Come with us."

He starts to walk and the area in which we are walking is very different. I hear the grass singing and the rocks having conversations.

The trees walk.

"The colors are so vivid here," I say.

"Yes, they are, Granddaughter," Grandmother says.

Before me appears our cabin at the river. That sweet river is in its most breathtaking state, rushing, rippling.

"Ah, it smells so good here."

The sun is bright and the sky is blue. I look beyond the house, at the magnificent mountains. The air is cool and fresh.

Grandfather steps up on the porch where there is a round table. He pulls out a chair for Grandmother and they sit down. Raven and I sit with them.

Grandfather says, "Hand down that bundle you're carrying."

I remember the lesson and I hand it right over to him. He takes the lizard bundle and says, "You are in the Will. You are deep inside the mind. You have followed the Rainbow Path, which is the soul, and you have come to a place where we can open the bundle of the lizard."

Grandmother looks at me and says, "Did you see the lightning bugs?"

I smile and say, "Yes, Grandmother. Their twinkling lights are such fun to see. I always loved those yellow and green lights. I wonder if everyone's seen a lightning bug, Grandmother."

She drops her eyes and says, "Not everyone. No, but they will in time.

They will take time to look for the spirit lights. They will take time to find the places where it's healthy and the lightning bug still lives."

"If they make it here, "Grandfather says, "they will always see the spirit lights." He points and the trees shimmer with color. Each leaf, each needle, each limb has spirit lights twinkling on it..

My heart is filled with joy. Grandfather opens the bundle and as he does, millions of sparks of color shoot out and dance in the sky. The bundle vibrates and trembles with color.

"Because of your belief, you have followed and you have found spiritual enlightenment. Because you seek out the way of the Rainbow Medicine Wheel and follow your Vision, you walk with old. You walk with the ways of the lizard."

I watch Raven watching the colors flutter and shimmer. Each sparkle reflects thousands of shades of color as they flitter past us. In Grandmother and Grandfather's hair are spirit lights, twinkling stars.

"The lightning bugs have brought you to the spirit lights—the fullest and most powerful acknowledgment of the Will of Great Spirit. You must remember Mother and Father Earth. You must remember the ways of Grandmother/Grandfather Wolf and rejoice in the face of Great Spirit."

I remember the silver and gold faces—plump, rounded, gentle— with their small pug noses and soft, twinkling lights for eyes.

"Is this all there is, Grandmother?" I ask.

Grandmother laughs and says, "No, dear. There is the Strength. There is the sound. There are the ways of Sweet Medicine," and her eyes sparkle.

"There are still teachings—and they are the strong teachings—the ones of the Seven Sacred Directions. Come with me and I will show you something."

She walks down the steps and we head toward the river.

"I think of him," I say, "his dark eyes, his deep voice."

"I know," Grandmother says. "But, he is not gone. He is your heart. The blueness, the depth, the Truth, and the knowing of love. That is one of the sacred directions. You will learn lessons."

She points and alongside the river are seven colored flowers. They had a shimmering aura about them that glistens and vibrates. Their colors are opalescent.

"Sweet Medicine calls, listen."

I hear the wind, but beyond the wind I hear voices.

"Smoke, the fire, the earth, Sincerity, Honesty," the voices get soft, the wind still. I feel as if I could step off into the color and walk on it..

Grandmother puts her hands on my shoulders and says, "Wait. I must tell you something before you go."

I look at her. "I have found the answers to the Will of Great Spirit, I tell her. "I know inner peace."

"Yes," she says, "You are home. Where the Blue-Eyed Raven and I are one."

"I know, Grandmother, I see now. I have no pain. I have the answers to my search."

"Right, tell me what you know," she says.

"Dark Eyes and all the teachings of King Coyote are the South part of the Blue Road. We all as humankind have to walk the wheel of life to learn the lessons. Lessons deal with our emotions in life and they have a purpose, as Dark Eyes has had in my life. When we have fear, we all want answers. And, as humankind, we blame others instead of looking at the Truth. We want to find a Reason when we don't understand. I have found the way to the Will of the Creator—it is in the soul. As we are open to the spirit and the ways of the spirit, we will know the answers in the lesson of forgiveness.

"That's right, Granddaughter, Forgiveness is the voice of the soul. The humankind spend a lot of time being lost. The answers are easy," she says. "The teachings of the wheel all lead to the Truth—home."

**I hear the howl of the wolf calling me back.**

# THE TEACHINGS OF WILL—MAGPIE

In the teaching of Will you are faced with your deepest questions. You are facing the facts in life. You will see that you are Spirit, Emotions, and Body. Your will is the Balance between the light and the dark. It is bringing you to the point where you have to believe, where you have to live a life of strong beliefs or live with ignorance. Will gives you Choice. The outcome will be the point at which you face the fact that you have made a good Choice, or that you have acted with anger and fear, because of what you have been taught.

Will is the medicine of flow and freedom. It is your Choice or decision, the facts or purpose. Will is your connection to Understanding the spiritual purposes in your daily life. When you are at peace with life, you can see that all in life is the will of a force outside your self. When the will of Great Spirit is hard to understand, you have choices that can make life easier.

The totem of Will is the magpie. The words for the magpie are the words of Will: prophecy, communication, intelligence, and discernment. When you know and practice the action of Will you will have the ability to see and direct your outcomes in life, as well make your own way in the world. You have control when you apply Will to your life. Within Will is your natural intelligence.

As you go about your life, you must know that you have ability and intelligence. These two points within Will are the major factors that open the door to Success and achievement. Will is soul Energy, which means it comes from Great Spirit/Grandmother/Grandfather/Creator/God. Will is pure Energy with positive ability—what your brain is capable of, the expression of your abilities.

> **Example:** *As you see things in life like death and sadness, you can look at them as events that happen and know that you have feelings about them. You must come to a Balance in those feelings. You have the Choice of letting the event bother you or accepting it and moving on. You can journal or pray or seek counsel and accept.*

Through belief and spirit you can will yourself to do or be anything you wish. Will is truly magical; it holds the Energy and ability for you to make a Choice and have your mind's desire.

Aho!

## SOUL RETRIEVAL

When you study spirituality, it includes all beliefs. The first step in understanding the soul is to have an open mind. An open mind means that you are always open to hear the voice of spirit. The voice of spirit may come through others. It may be teachings of religions that are very, very old.

I have found through my spiritual upbringing and through the wonderful teachers that I have experienced that we are only what we're taught—unless we embrace the voice of our mind and go within our spirit. We can do this through spiritual journey work, by having a Vision and following the Vision, by gathering Knowledge, sorting through it, and accepting the medicine words—applying Color, Energy, Prayer, Courage, Understanding, Knowledge, and Will as the soul path.

In our lives, we hear a lot about the soul, and I can remember wanting to know what a soul was. I had a very wise teacher say to me once, "It's connected to your foot," and he looked me at me and smiled. Well, as the years went on, I realized he wasn't too far away from the Truth. Our soul is our spiritual pathway, and in spirit we walk on it with our spirit feet.

As I have searched for the answer, many people have told me that the soul is good energy. Many have told me that it is your spirit. Many have told me that it something that you can lose to the Devil. As a spiritual teacher, working with Grandmother/Grandfather/Great Spirit/Creator/God, it's my Responsibility to teach what a soul is.

**Soul definition, according to Wolf Moondance:**

The soul is principle. It is the ability to feel and have thought. It is distinctly separate from spirit and the physical. It is the seat of human feelings, the home of courage, the embodiment of quality. To me, the soul starts with pure Energy and there are seven movements:

**1. Clean.** This means there is Balance. The Energy is free from any negative charge. There are no emotions of physicality connected to the Energy.

**2. Open.** This means having no set belief or negative concept. There needs to be an open mind, free from controlled or negative thinking.

**3. Spirit.** The soul, in its purest form, is the beginning of spirit. From the Red Road, which is the soul of Great Spirit, comes each point of Energy. As each point becomes Energy, it becomes a spirit. The spirit has a pathway and that is soul.

**4. Knowing.** In pure Energy, knowing is the resonance of vibration, harmony, peace, Tranquility, solitude, and Sincerity. Within these energies is the Strength of the soul.

**5. Fearless.** In pure Energy, there is no emotion. There are forms of resonance, perpetual motion, existence, infinity, and eternity. Those are the structures of Energy. There are no challenges and no needs. There is no time—only being, existence, comprehension, and development.

**6. Balance.** Pure Energy is balanced. When you know your goals and spiritual beliefs, know that you are both physical and spirit, know that you may have an imbalance in your brain, you are living with wholeness and forgiveness.

**7. Complexity.** Everything exists within pure Energy. There will be diversity, Change, abruptness, destruction, and reformation.

To understand the soul, you need to accept these seven movements of pure Energy. You cannot add to them. Don't try to think about them in any physical way. You can compare the seven movements to some earthly Visions, some earthly matter that makes them more understandable, such as liquid, the sky, the air we breathe, the fire, the structure of the earth, the embodiment of a human being. It takes the seven movements of pure Energy to be able to understand the complexity of the soul.

The soul is a simple thing—the pathway of spirit, the pure Energy that allows the spirit to take form and come into material existence as a being. There is a separation between spirit and soul, just as there is a difference between the mind and the brain, the brain being physical and the mind spiritual. The spirit can be seen as physical in the spirit realm—a willowy, watery form, for example—while the soul is pure Energy.

As humans we live in the middle world, which is the realm of reality. The spirit lives in the upper world and also in the lower world. Our soul is the most precious part of our existence because it is pure Energy. As humans we can only really understand our soul through shamanic journey. Through shamanic journey we can breathe and relax, allowing our mind to open and look for the familiar path. Any pathway is the soul. If we are looking for the soul within ourselves, we can simply look at the path. The complexity of the soul is infinite, and that means that your path may change. The unique thing about shamanic journey is that it brings everything into form. If you are open, clear, balanced, and acting out of Creativity, through shamanic journey you will be able to see every aspect of your soul.

The soul could be a pathway by the ocean, which would be the symbol of ultimate Strength for the ocean is the strongest Power. To interpret your soul, you need to be able to understand the elements of Earth Mother. If you were to see a pathway made of pure, clean dirt, it would reflect the Power of earth, which is bringing forth, growing, enabling, nurturing. When you start looking at the different pathways, you will begin to comprehend how complex the soul is.

A healthy soul consists of:

1. A healthy body.
2. An Understanding of life, its (1) purpose, (2) principles, (3) values, (4) Respect and spiritual Understandings.
Spiritual Understandings are:
(1) allowing yourself to interact with dreamtime,
(2) allowing yourself to go on vision quests and to have a personal Vision and an understanding of that Vision,
(3) an active Prayer life,
(4) discipline and obedience to the suggestions from your guides and interactions through Prayer.

## UNDERSTANDING THE DESTRUCTION OF A SOUL

As a human two-legged, you can lose touch with your soul. You do this by having anger, low self esteem, and through:

1. Addictions.
   a) Alcohol
   b) Drugs
   c) Food
   d) Sex
   e) Money
   f) Work
2. Long illness.
3. Loss of family connection.
4. Sibling anger.
5. Stealing.
6. Lying.
7. Unwanted pregnancies.
8. Rape.
9. Molestation.
10. Self-lies.
11. Denial.
12. Death of a loved one.
13. Death of a pet.
14. Grief.
15. Broken heart.

16. Divorce.
17. Broken relationships.
18. Car crash or other harsh physical accident.
19. A lack of forgiveness.

These are many ways in which your aura can be severely torn, which will cause your Energy grids to expand or contract. This will affect your chakra system and create the dark spots that I call chug holes or wash-outs in the path.

To have healthy soul Energy, you need to understand your personality. Connecting with your inner peace lessons, standing strong in the Knowledge that you have spirituality and a Vision, and providing stable peace and limits within your life, will help your soul to be rich and full.

Aho.

## CEREMONY OF SOUL RECOVERY

You need to view your soul as your connection to Grandfather/Grandmother/Great Spirit. You need to understand that your soul is your sacred path, and that the sacred path is the Energy that allows your existence to manifest. Your soul supplies the Energy for the manifestation of matter. Harshness, disruption, despair, disease, dis-ease are ways that the soul loses spiritual Energy. Soul retrieval can be done in many ways, but I teach it through shamanic journey. Since the soul is spiritual Energy, the work is done through interactional thought, which is a mild hypnotic relaxation through shamanic journey that allows you to experience your soul, thereby increasing the Energy in your human existence. The following shamanic journey is a soul-retrieval exercise.

Find a tranquil place where you can relax. Sit quietly, keep yourself warm and comfortable, and understand that you must not fall asleep during this exercise. It is important that you come back from your shamanic journey and journal your feelings and thoughts, so you will need a journal and pen for this exercise, plus your smudging tools.

Also, you may be suffering from a lot of different conditions in your life that require counseling, and there are many kinds of counselors and therapists. I recommend that you get one who specializes in the problems that you are dealing with. Look at the situations that cause disruption or abuse to your soul and find a counselor in the area of drug abuse, alcohol abuse, sexual abuse or sexual disorders, food addiction, eating disorders, sleeping disorders, or gambling. When your soul is affected, your Energy from the Good Red Road, the path of Great Spirit, will be depleted. When the Energy of the soul is depleted, it affects your spirit and can even cause terminal depletion of the spirit, because the mental condition of the human two-legged can diminish to the point of death. Mental illness, mental disturbance, is serious. Unbalanced anger and harbored grudges can cause severe chemical imbalance and permanent damage to the brain.

## SHAMANIC SOUL-RETRIEVAL JOURNEY

Smudge first by lighting your sage or sweet grass and blowing the fire out. Fan the smoke around your body clockwise four times to clear your spirit.

Sit very still, in a comfortable position, and relax. Take four deep breaths in and out, and continue breathing deeply. Look straight ahead and with your mind's eye, the eye of the spirit, look at the colors that are before you. If you can not see a color, then consciously place a color in your mind. Record that color in your journal. When you come back from your journey, look up the information about the color in the back of the book, for it will tell you the treatment and the lesson you need to understand to begin your soul retrieval.

Continue breathing deeply and look for a colored path. If you cannot see a colored path, put a colored path there. See it. When you come back, record the color of the path in your journal. This is the medicine color and the color of the lessons that your soul needs in order to heal the disorders in your physical existence.

Walk on the path. You will come to an area that you call your center. There you will find a comfortable place to sit down. It might be leaning against a tree, on a rock or a park bench or a stool, or a chair. Sit there. In your spirit, take in a deep breath, and as you do, visualize the color red. Blow out the color red, and you will see a red path. Breathe in again, and then blow out the color orange, and you will see an orange path. Continue doing this with yellow, green, blue, purple, and burgundy, breathing in the color and blowing out the color, until you see a rainbow path.

Visualize those colors very strongly. Watch them as they begin to spiral. They lift up in the air and turn to soft snowflakes of all seven colors. The snow falls gently on your spirit presence. It coats your body with rainbow Energy. Breathe in and out fourteen times, and relax.

The snow now becomes silver and you are coated with silver Energy. Breathe in and out four times. For the fifth breath, breathe in the silver Energy and blow it out, and you will see a strong silver path in front of you. There will be a bright blue sky, strong yellow sunlight, and the silver path will glisten and shimmer. Before you, everything will take on a bright silver-white light, so bright that you can see only the brightness. Sit in that brightness and breathe in and out.

When you have taken twenty-eight breaths, open your eyes. You will feel Energy pulsating in your body. This is the shamanic journey of soul-retrieval, taking back the Energy of your spirit, strengthening your chakras, balancing the colors in your aura.

When you have finished this journey, write in your journal the colors that you saw, the feelings that you felt, the things you had trouble balancing in your mind. Any time you feel weakened and or fearful, use this technique. Remember that soul retrieval is done through balancing Energy, but to repair the damage that has taken place within the brain, you must come to a Balance and an Understanding of the abuse that has taken place in your body. The main thing you need to understand when you are working with rejuvenating your soul and balancing your mind and your brain, is that you cannot blame. You cannot look back and have regrets. You cannot wish things had been a different way. You have to accept what has been as the best possible thing that could have happened for your future Growth, and go on from there.

Remember, as long as you are physically alive you have the opportunity to experience and learn the lessons of physical life. I recommend that you do the soul retrieval exercise no less than every fourth day. It is important to keep a strong soul.

Aho.

## AN EXERCISE OF SOUL RETRIEVAL

As we walk as human two-leggeds, we experience abuses. There is not a day you live that abuse doesn't take place and affect you in one way or another. If a soul is affected by abuse, it starts to have black spots in it. and there is a need to fill the spot with Color.

To retrieve your soul, ask yourself the following questions. You can write about them in your journal as often as you need to, until you find the answers that bring Color back into your damaged soul. When a soul has black spots, it becomes weakened. It is my theory that mental anguish brings about a lot of disease and ill health.

1. What brings peace to your life?
2. What is your Strength?
3. What have you lost in your life?
4. What is your emptiness?
5. What is your deepest fear?
6. What lies do you harbor?
7. What do you dislike?
8. What is the worst thing you have done in your life?
9. What makes it the worst thing? Who says?
10. What do you not know and would like to know?
11. Do you wish harm on anyone? Whom?
12. Why would you wish to harm any one? What can you do to get over the anger?.
13. Who have you harmed in your life?
14. Was there mental illness in your family? If so, who and what? Have you spoken to anyone about your mental health and how you need to understand and treat the brain? If not, why not?
15. What are your strong likings?
16. What do you love, and why?
17. What is the self? Explain.
18. What is your spiritual connection? What spiritual teachings guide you?
19. What color is your favorite and why?
20. Are there any colors you don't like? If your answer to this question is yes, look at those colors and read from the medicines in the back of the book. Apply those actions to your life and understand that you need to come to like all the colors for your soul to be strong.

Write about these issues in your journal until you feel everything is resolved. There are many more things you can do to retrieve your soul. It takes time and, in some cases, a soul retrieval counselor. Often a general counselor can help you unlock feelings that are tearing away at your Energy system.

What is the importance of soul retrieval? It simply allows you to have the fullest connection to Grandmother/Grandfather/Great Spirit that you can have. If you are working on your inner self, wanting to have the wholeness of the self, you need to examine your belief systems. Are they yours or did they come from someone else and you are simply doing what you were told? You need to know where your belief systems come from. Did you think them up on your own? Did you find them of your own free Will? Do you agree with your belief systems?

One way to do this is to ask yourself the following questions:

1. What do you believe about marriage?
2. What do you believe about death and grief?
3. What do you believe about owning a home?
4. What do you believe about the government?
5. What do you believe about education?
6. What do you believe about the word "family"?
7. What do you believe about divorce?
8. What are your beliefs about religion?
9. What do you know to be true?
10. Do you believe in evil?
11. What is ugly to you?
12. Do you believe in spirituality or religion? Is there a difference ?
13. Do you know where you go when you die?
14. Do you know where you were before you were born?
15. What do you think UFOs exist? Why would you think there are beings other than us?
16. Do you believe that all things are friendly or do you believe that there may be evil hiding behind things that seem to be friendly?
17. Do you know the difference between being drunk and being filled with the spirit?
18. Do you believe in the spirit world? If so, do you have any Proof?
19. Do you have a personal Vision? If so, can you interpret it and apply it to your life?
20. Do you believe that you are in control of your life and understand it— or are you a victim of life, waiting for others to answer your questions?

These are good questions for you to work with to have a solid Understanding of who is in control of your mind. Make sure you are always in control of your own mind—and that it is not your brain that is in control, just acting out of normal physical power. It is interesting to realize it is possible for the brain to be in total control of your life, while your mind is void of action, trapped in a physical entity.

Aho.

# THE LESSON OF INNER PEACE— THE LIGHTNING BUG

Understanding inner peace brings Balance to your physical existence. When you grasp the lesson of inner peace, you have determination, you have the ability to feel and act with joy. You have the capability of Understanding life's harsh lessons and feeling its sweet successes, and you will find that you have a strong spirit.

It is important to realize that your physical brain can be chemically out of balance from poor eating habits, poor rest habits, overworking habits, being unbalanced in your fears, harboring hate and anger, wishing harm to others, thinking judgmental thoughts, and acting with weakness. It is important, when you are learning the lesson of inner peace, that you check with yourself on a daily basis and communicate with your medicines.

Bringing about the lesson of inner peace is a Balance of Color in your life. When you have learned the lesson of inner peace, you will like every color in the rainbow. You will have no one color you like more than another. You will not say, oh, I don't like yellow, or I don't like orange, or I can't stand red, I only like blue or I only like green. When you only like one or two colors, you have a lot of inner turmoil. The way you can tell what turmoil you have is by which color you don't like. Look at the colors you don't like, and check out the words under the Color definitions in the back of the book. You'll see the medicines you need to apply to your life and the lessons you need to learn from the colors you don't like.

> **Example:** *You don't like blue—then you are in need of learning the medicine of Truth, the medicine of Healing, the medicine of Proof, the medicine of Understanding, as well as the lessons that go along with the color blue. You will see color for the spiritual energy that it is.*

The human two-legged is a lot like the lightning bug. As long as the lightning bug can flash color, it is alive. When it can no longer flash its light, its physical existence is over. When, as human two-leggeds, we are sad and angry, we cannot use the Colors, and we miss out on the joys of life. The fears and anger we harbor can keep us from expressing our true nature, and bring us to the point of sickness and even death.

We as human two-leggeds spend an awful lot of time in turmoil, mental and emotional disturbance, mental illness, We walk with a tremendous lack of inner peace. When we obtain inner peace, we Balance our lives with sacredness, with Ceremony, with spiritual Understanding, and joy. We do that by applying the medicines in our lives. Medicines are Colors and Colors have definition. Inner peace walks hand in hand with Will. Remember that it is your Will to remain in disease, disconnected from your goals, walking in a fearful way with a lack of exercise, in imbalance, with anger and fear.

It takes a lot of work in your physical life to have inner peace. It all starts with acceptance.

I once taught a lesson about inner peace, and I would like to share it with you now. The word "perfect" expresses inner peace, and perfect means "everything is okay just the way it is." If you can stay in that frame of mind, you are beginning to walk in acceptance. Then you can set goals through your intentions and bring about inner peace. But achievement is not inner peace. Perfect is inner peace. And perfect is okay just the way it is.

When we obtain inner peace, at that moment we stand in the center, we stand centered, in Balance with Great Spirit on the Good Red Road.

Aho.

# 11 ◆ SWEET MEDICINE

I take off my medicine coat, hold my black hat in my hand, and watch them go. Those seven have been something. They are wonderful students, with me a long time, and here I stand in the East gate ready to go again. They'll take a rest and they'll be back. They have seen the East section, the South, the West, and the North section, and they have learned their medicines from each one. Now they are ready to go to the center, to study Sweet Medicine.

In the old days for the people of Turtle Island, Sweet Medicine was a teaching based on the sun dance. In Rainbow Medicine it is speaking to Grandmother/Grandfather/Great Spirit/Creator/God. We will take a walk in to the center of the wheel and study the teachings of the seven sacred stars/Colors in the center of the wheel. In Sweet Medicine we hear teachings about Creation and the ways of Great Spirit and the upper world.

"So how does it feel to understand the soul? Are you ready to close the door on me? I hear a deep voice say.

I hear the rushing water of the river, smell the sweet scent of flowers. I see a huge old cottonwood tree and standing there is Dark Eyes.

"Did you forget me. I know you live a busy life. Are we over?" He smiles.

"You know I have learned a lot from the north section of the wheel. I know that I have to face all the emotions and feelings the brain and mind have. I know that there are feelings I can't live with out on the Earth Mother and you are one of them. The feelings are deep and there is nowhere to run from them," I say.

"Would you want to live a life without romance or passion?" he asks.

"I don't want to miss anything in life—that's why I love the Rainbow Medicine Wheel. Everything is in the wheel, the wheel is everything." I say.

"Yep, I guess what makes it all hard are the blaming and guilt that people place on each other. It causes things to get all muddy and makes you worry," he says. "There is so much to life and as we walk the wheel we get a close and personal look at all of it. How about a dance on the river—catch me if you can!"

He jumps from one stone to another. I follow, we dance the river in the early morning sun.

"The important factor to remember is when you come to the medicine wheel you are free from limits, and marriage is of the soul. It is true that your soul mate is part of wholeness and completion," he says as he crosses the river. "But who said that the doors of love close?

"There is a journey ahead of you that teaches the voices of Great Spirit. A place where all just is and no titles or ways of thinking influence humankind. It is in the center of the wheel that we are in pure spirit and we are free, with no limits or expectations. Yes, Sweet Medicine, the voice of Creator."

I take a deep breath in and out, and I relax. I look into the bright sun. I begin to see a path and step out on it. It is hot white sand. I start walking into the blazing sun, leaving winter behind me. I go past the medicines and through the lessons and I am standing in the brightest white light. I cannot see anything but bright light—it is blinding. I look hard, beyond the light, and I see someone standing there.

"Hello?" I say. "Hello, can you hear me?"

There is no reply. The spirit comes closer. It is small, maybe five feet (1.5m) tall, round and heavy-set, and the light dances over its presence. There is the dazzle and glimmer of sparks all around it.

A strong vibration extends towards me. I feel the glow of light from the spirit touch my face. The spirit makes itself clear. I can see that it is similar to humankind in form and body, but it is not a human because it is neither male nor female. It has a face and hands and feet, and it wears a beautiful colored robe that shimmers in the light. Stars flutter from the bottom of the cloth and dance on the ground. The spirit has strands of stars for hair. Its face is old, ancient—a very wrinkled face. It has large ears and dimples in its cheeks. It holds out its hand and in it is a small glass bottle, burgundy in color. With its other hand, the spirit opens the bottle and color flies from it. I hear the sounds of many voices singing. I hear drumming and flutes and the bells of dancers. All this sound and vibration rushes from the bottle. Stars are flying everywhere and circling the spirit.

The space around me becomes very comfortable. There is soft, green grass and a pond with a fountain in the center, and colored water is shooting in the air—soft colors of blues, greens, and lavenders come from the fountain.

"Hello," the spirit says. "I have been waiting on you." The spirit speaks in a monotone. "You will like it here. We have much to teach you and you will have much to share with your students."

"Who are you?" I ask.

The spirit replies, "I am Wrinkle-face."

That's a good name, for there are many, many wrinkles in the spirit's face. As I am closer now, I see its eyebrows are stars. It is also wearing a belt made of stars on its dazzling gown. The belt is tied and the two ends hang down in front. On one end is a sun and on the other a moon.

The wind picks up softly, a gentle breeze blows all around me.

"Where am I?" I ask Wrinkle-face.

"You are beyond the sun in the land of ancestors. We have called you here to be in the center. We need you to explain the teachings of Sweet Medicine. This is a time when the students will gather and learn about

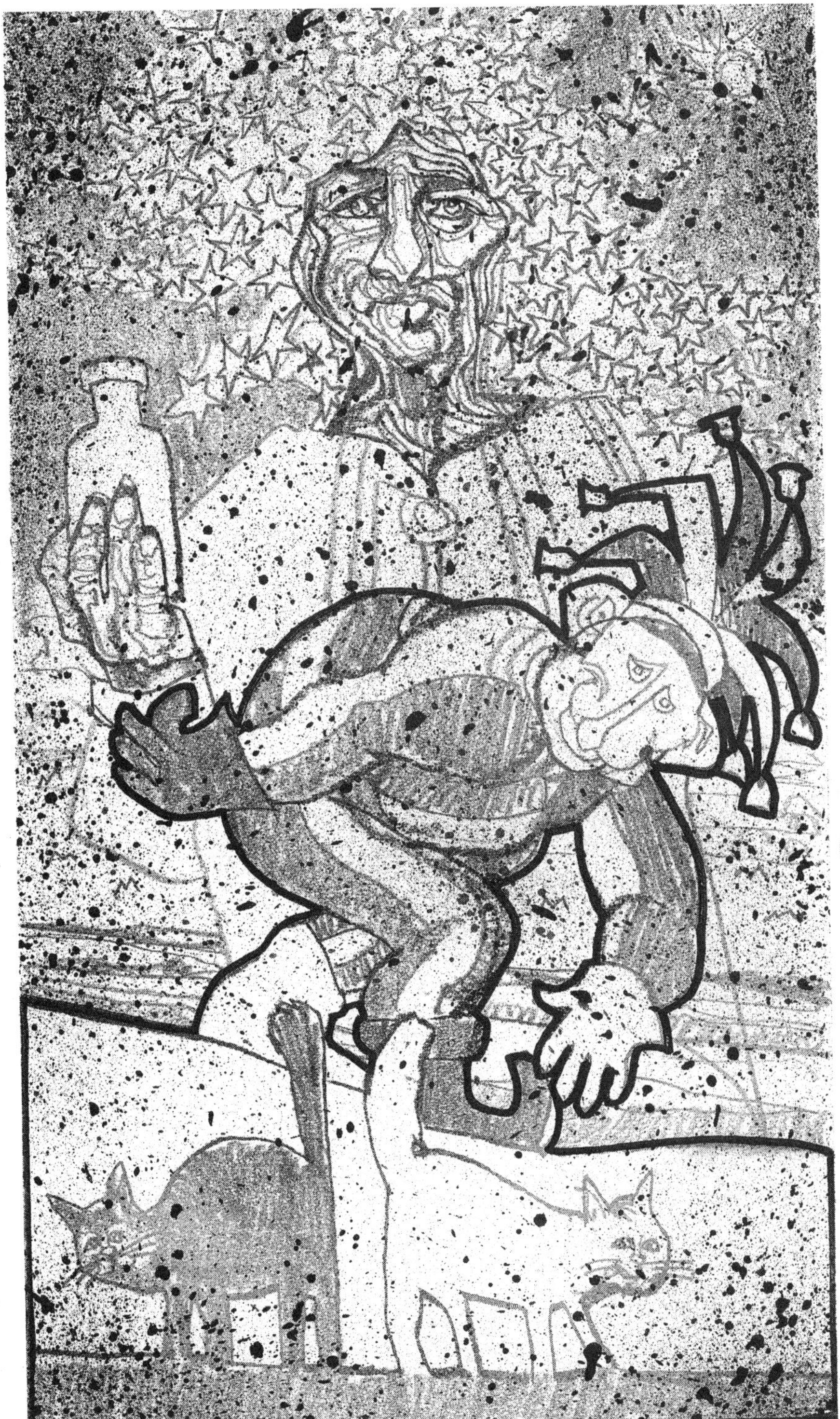

Accountability. They will understand Responsibility, Sincerity, Honesty, Respect, Commitment and Mystery."

When Wrinkle-face says "Mystery," the fountain shoots stars high into the air. The sky is a deep, rich blue and the stars are bouncing against the trees, the rocks, the ground—everything. They scatter in all directions.

Another spirit comes tumbling in, rolling head over heels like a ball. It is dressed in a jester's costume with a pointed rainbow hat with seven bells on the ends of it. Its shirt is red, orange, and yellow. Its belt is green. Its pants are burgundy, blue, and purple. Its shoes curl up at the toes and stars cascade off the points. One shoe is black, one white. The spirit wears gloves, black and white, and on the ends of each finger are seven colored stars. The spirit stands a little over two feet (.6m) tall. Its eyes glisten—they are turquoise. Its nose is long and pointed, its ears big and rounded. Its chin is long. It seems young, yet I know it is ancient.

"Yes, Wolf. This is Zanday. Zanday is the spirit of happiness. It has come to show you your way, where you will be staying here. Please follow Zanday."

Wrinkle-face extends its hand and points to the hill.

I leave with Zanday, who begins to roll and tumble and motions for me to follow. Great! I will now roll like a jester and act like a jokester. I tumble and become a ball and I follow. The motion is fun. I have not done it in a long time. I land at the end of the porch of a small yellow house. There is a swing on the porch with a big white cat lying on it. Zanday opens the door and a black cat runs out. It rubs up against my legs and purrs.

"These are your friends. They are here for you. They know you like them and they will tell you the stories of Sweet Medicine. You have things to share." Zanday hands me my drum bag. "Play. Play to the sun."

Poof, the spirit disappears in an array of glistening color. Sparks dance and flash in all directions. I look beyond where Zanday had been and I see the sun setting. I take out my drum and I begin to play. A wonderful, fresh feeling comes over me. I can hear my drum echoing alongside many other drums. I smell the wonderful aroma of campfires burning. Up the path comes Wrinkle-face and I keep drumming. Wrinkle-face sits on the swing with the white cat. I drum until the sun disappears.

"We're glad that you've come, Wolf. It is time to teach the center. It is time to tell about the sacred spiral and share the teachings of harmonics, as well as the Knowledge of the chakras. It is time to teach the secrets of the Balance within the sacred tunnels of energy. We will talk of numbers and their frequencies, and how the colors teach the days."

The spirit is sitting cross-legged on the swing and nodding. "Hmmm, yes. The teachings are good and we will start tomorrow."

I hear a soft rattle—the drums still playing. I sit in Sweet Medicine. The rainbow of colors begins to fade into darkness.

A soft voice speaks in the wind. It is a woman's voice and sounds like a song.

"Yes, Wolf, it is a song—the song of the wheel's center, the voice of Great Spirit," the voice says. "Humankind are in need of the teachings of Mystery. They are called to learn the ways of Sweet Medicine. That is the ability to speak to Great Spirit and hear the teachings of the inner spirit of the self. You know, a good talk with Grandmother/Grandfather is what all humankind need to understand during their time on the Earth Mother."

I see a soft mist of color, blues and oranges and yellows all around me. It is cool and fresh. It energizes me and I feel uplifted. I sit on a large rock. I don't want to miss anything I'm about to hear.

"Yes, this is the way of Sweet Medicine. You want Accountability and Responsibility. You feel the Sincerity. You feel the Honesty and Respect, Commitment, and Mystery—these are the medicine words of Sweet Medicine. They are part of the seven sacred directions. As you take your students to the center of the medicine wheel, they will be open to the sweet side of the self. This is a connection to a wonderful teacher, Granny Smith," the voice says.

I hear something behind me. I turn and there is a cute little Grandmother. She is short and a little heavy. She has on a white shirt, a skirt of many colors, and a green apron that goes around her neck. I can just barely see her tiny tennis shoes peeking out from under the long skirt. Her small face is wrinkled and she has a pug noise and little half glasses that sit on the end of her nose. She has big soft brown eyes and gray and white hair all done up in a bun on top of her head.

"What you look at, girl? "She asks.

"You, who might you be? "I reply.

"Well, a dear friend of your Grandmother Wolf, first of all, but to you—a guide for your journey," she says. I notice she has a mixing bowl in her hands.

"What are you mixing?" I say.

"Time—mixing you some time. You don't have much and they are awaiting, the ones with the big noise. They are the ones with the tests and questions. You'll see," she says. "I'm Granny Smith, sweetie. I will lead you to the voice of the Great One, in the center. You must be ready. I have been told you understand the Rainbow Medicine wheel and walk with the name White Wolf. Hey girl, if you look in a pond, what do you look like?" she grins. "You are one who teaches the Truth of the center. When we are done, your students and many others will know the secrets and ways of Prayer. It will be our joy to help humankind to talk with Great Spirit and understand they have no need to fear. That's why you need time. Time for them to not have fear." She laughs.

I feel a strong love and can smell apple pie. What a wonderful Granny!

**I hear the howl of the wolf calling me back.**

## SWEET MEDICINE—THE CENTER

Sweet Medicine is in the center of the Rainbow Medicine Wheel. It helps us understand Creation and our personal relationship with Grandmother/Grandfather/Great Spirit/Creator/God. Sweet Medicine beckons us to come and listen, to gather the Knowledge of why there are four directions and what the Ceremonies of fire, earth, wind, and air are.

Sweet Medicine beckons us to understand the seven sacred directions, to go into the underworld, and to get a clear understanding of where what we call evil comes from. It is calling to give us the sweetness of sacred living and to teach us how to apply Rainbow Medicine to our daily lives. Sweet Medicine shows us a place where the deer graze in their gentleness after they have brought the Prayer ties to Grandmother/Grandfather/Great Spirit/Creator/God.

Sweet Medicine teaches us Accountability, Responsibility, Sincerity, Honesty, Respect, Commitment, and Mystery. Each one of us lives with a particular harmonic frequency and exists within the Energy flows from sunrise to sunrise.

In Sweet Medicine we walk the circle of the sun and perform the

Ceremony of the four movements of the day. Sweet Medicine helps each of us understand our daily lessons and the medicine we each need to treat the lessons of life. In Sweet Medicine we are open to the Colors and the teachings of the stars. We listen to the star people in spirit and each one of us will receive the teachings we need to follow the Rainbow Path—the Good Red Road.

Aho.

# PRAYER BOWL

A prayer bowl is a sacred object that holds your Prayers, wishes, thoughts, dreams, intentions, and sacredness. It is a place to keep these feelings and allow them to move on to other dimensions. A Prayer bowl is used to bring sacredness into a room without causing a lot of attention. There are times when you need your Prayer bowl and want to be discreet about it. It is good to have one in your workplace. While co-workers and others think it is just a decoration, for you it is a sacred connection—a magical tool to refer to when in need of Prayer.

A Prayer bowl has dirt placed in the bottom of it and a feather that ticks up in the middle. The feather holds within it the sacred Power of the animal that gave it to you. You need to choose a feather from a power animal that you relate to—an eagle, an owl, a raven, a hawk, a crow, a turkey, or any other small bird, such as a blue jay, a magpie, a goose, or a chicken. It is good to use turkey feathers to represent the feathers of any endangered birds, such as hawks, eagles, or owls.

You will need a crystal for your Prayer bowl. It can be anything from clear quartz for focusing energy, to a hematite to Balance and ground Energy.

**Tools:** *A small bowl that you like, preferably oblong and flat—you can make it of clay, if you wish; a feather of a bird with which you feel a strong connection; 2 crystals; either garden dirt, black in color, or sand; a white candle and matches; smudge bowl and sage.*

Select a place in which you can sit and bring your Prayer bowl forth without being disturbed.

To bring forth your Prayer bowl, start by lighting your candle. Take the bowl, with the Understanding that the bowl represents the circle of sacred life. Place dirt in the bottom of the bowl until the bowl is half filled. The dirt represents your commitment to the Earth Mother and gratitude for the life that she brings forth to all people.

Take your feather and gaze at it. Think of the bird that has given you this gift, which allows you to be connected to the air. Stick the end of the feather in the dirt so that the feather stands up in the center of your bowl. Place the crystals, with their points facing up, on the right and left side of the feather. The crystals represent the Good Red Road, the road of spirit. Now gaze at the feather again and think about the bird it came from or the bird it represents. Think about how the bird sees the world and how it is free. Look at the dirt and feel its natural empowerment, its grounding force. Feel the strength of the earth underneath you and give thanks to the Earth Mother. Think of the bowl representing the circle, the Sacred Circle of Life. Feel the Energy of the spiraling circle.

Breathe in and out and feel the Energy of the sacred rainbow spiraling around the circle. Connect with the crystals and feel their Energy. What do they mean to you? Visualize the crystals as stone people filled with Knowledge representing the Good Red Road, connecting with your soul, running Energy from you to Great Spirit and from Great Spirit to you.

Say a Prayer: feel its Energy passing through the bowl. and be grateful that you are heard. Understand that Prayer is Sweet Medicine, and that it allows you to have communication with Grandmother/Grandfather/Great Spirit. Know that your Prayer bowl is Sweet Medicine.

Blow out the candle and place your bowl on a window ledge where it can feel the sun, where the feather can connect to the life of the birds, and where the crystal can sense its brother and sister rocks and the dirt that is connected to the earth. Use your Prayer bowl any time that you want to hear the Sweet Medicine of Prayer. Sit with your Prayer bowl and feel the goodness within Prayer.

Aho.

## CEREMONY OF CLEARING THE MIND

This is a good Ceremony to perform when you feel extremely stressed or have a lot going on in your thoughts. You will need a quiet place to sit and your journal and pen to record what you have felt when you are through with the Ceremony.

Sit comfortably and feel that you are safe and warm. Hold your head up with your chin straight. Breathe in and out through your nose four times. Continue breathing softly and listen. Notice whether you are thinking thoughts or if your mind is quiet. If there are a lot of thoughts in your mind and a lot is worrying you, you will need to visualize a very, very faint blue color—so faint that it is almost white. Breathe in and out softly. Do that four times and on the fourth breath take a deep breath in, and then relax and let the breath out. See the color now becoming sky blue.

Breathe in and out four times. See the color become a deep, rich blue—a crayon blue. Breathe in and out four times. Now see the color become a rich, vibrant blue etched in silver. In your mind's eye, pull that color in through your nose and fill your whole mind with it. Feel the color gently comforting your brain and relaxing your mind. Allow it to run down your spinal column and all through your body. Continue breathing in and out, filling your body with that beautiful blue color until every muscle, every fiber, every cell, and every tissue in your body is totally blue.

Continue the soft breathing and relax, sitting very still and allowing the blue color to bathe your body. Feel the color coming out the soles of your feet and the palms of your hands. Let the color shoot out your ears, out your nose, out your eyes and your mouth, and even your belly button, your reproductive area, and your buttocks. Have the color shoot out of every opening in your body. Feel the radiance of the Energy, the Understanding and Knowledge of the Color, and relax.

When you open your eyes, your mind will be clear and you will be filled with Truth and Healing Energy. You will have the Understanding that you need. You will be in Respect for yourself. Open your eyes and feel the clarity of your mind. Record in your journal how you feel.

I recommend that you use this exercise any time you feel overwhelmed. Aho.

## A CLOSING NOTE FROM WOLF MOONDANCE

As we walk in our physical life with the brain we have, we are looking at Mystery every day. I like what my mom taught me. "Your mysteries are the reason you get up tomorrow. To live and understand the purpose of the lesson of life."

As I live in the North part of the wheel, I know that Color is the strongest medicine we have. We are Energy whether we are matter or spirit. It is easy to be negative and feel fear and bring sadness to our lives. I have learned, from the Vision I walk with, that our mind speaks the Truth from Great Spirit. It is only fear that fuels our anger. It is easy to sit and do nothing, to blame and cry. Sickness comes when we call it. We should take a look at our Prayers and Understandings and see that the way for us to go is to work from inner peace.

To know is to heal. We have to listen to the lessons and walk with the teachings to open our lives to the sacred ways of Truth and Healing. The soul is the pathway to the spirit world and we each have a soul. Each of us is a magical being with all kinds of mysteries. Maybe one of them is to just be Grand.

I ask you what is "bad" in your life and where did it come from? Did you miss something someone was saying and that caused pain? Do you make your choices or do others? And why do others have the right to choose for you? When you are living your daily life, are you happy and do you feel complete? Or to you bring everything down and cause self-pain. It is your thoughts and only your thoughts that create your life. Be healthy mentally and let not a thing or a person get in the way of your best days.

One thing to remember about the North. You have a soul and it is the pathway to the stars. You have a Great Spirit/Creator/God who loves you just as you are. Take it easy on the brain and listen to the mind. You will hear the call of the wolf who speaks of the Rainbow Medicine path.

Aho !

# WOLF TEACHINGS

## COLORS

**Red**—Confidence, Strength, Nurture, Color, Accountability, patience, clarity, purpose, absolute, illumination, beginning, spring, spirit, enlightenment.

**Orange**—Balance, Success, Choice, Energy, Responsibility, unity, poise, obedience, correct, following, proceeding.

**Yellow**—Creativity, Vision, Ceremony, Prayer, Sincerity, original, discipline, life, ideal, solid.

**Green**—Growth, Beauty, Change, Quiet, Honesty, faith, account, action, flow, innocence.

**Blue**—Truth, Healing, Proof, Tranquility, Respect, sincerity, understanding, fact, solid, clear, introspection, within, calmness.

**Purple**—Wisdom, Power, Real, Knowledge, Committed, reason, sense, full, depth.

**Burgundy**—Impeccable, Great, Grand, Will, Mystery, worthy, worth, complete, spiritual, the Path.

**White/Silver**—Spiritual, all.

**Black/Gold**—Totality, wholeness, physical, monetary, mass, material, matter.

**Silver**—Soul.

**Gold**—Attraction, materialism, matter, humankind, physical.

## COLORS OF WOLF MEDICINE

**Red**—Color. Color is voice of the ancient one. It speaks of quality and substance, viewpoint, attitude, tone, appearance, and involvement.. Color ranges from skin tone to the hues of light, to light refraction, to pigment, to dyes that we make to color objects. Color can be paints. In its spiritual voice it is everything. Color is the strongest Confidence. It is your Strength, your ability to Nurture. It brings you into the fullest aspects of Accountability. With Color you can never go wrong. You can pick one and stand on it as a medicine. You can pick one and have it be a lesson. You can struggle and fight the Color of a lesson, but you will find that it will turn you around and set you strong on the path known as the soul. You will walk your path and connect with the all, with Grandmother/Grandfather/Great Spirit, and be fulfilled forever in light.

**Orange**—Energy. Energy is abundant. It leads others. It is expression and capacity, excellent, and forceful. Orange is the movement of the badger. It is Power that thrusts forth as the breath of life. Energy is the core of existence. It is the warmth in the hand of the old woman who touches the lonely child. It is the kiss that stays in your mind forever. It is the song that you hum on a good day. Energy is the capacity of all. It is the interweaving of what we know as the web of life.

**Yellow**—Prayer. Prayer is spiritual communication. It is the formula, the petition, the hope, and the chance. It is thanks and praise, bringing out. Prayer is the place you go where there is no place else that you can go. It is the action that gives you the perspective that there is a future. Prayer is compelling emotions, strong intense feelings. It is your ability to desire. Be careful what you pray for—you might get it. Prayer is sacred communication that allows the thoughts of Great Spirit to resonate with your spirit. It is within your self that answers come to you. Prayer opens doors to directions—the direction of enlightenment, the direction of innocence, the direction of introspection, and the direction of Knowledge.

**Green**—Courage. Courage is comprehension. It is intelligence and Knowledge, cooperation and agreement. It is interpretation and responsibilities. You might think that things are too hard and you might feel sorry for yourself and want to blame someone. You might want to harbor anger and turn your back. Courage spins you around like the wind, setting you firmly on a path, and tells you to listen to the voice of your soul. Courage allows you to hear the voices of the medicines. It tells you that you must learn your lessons and walk in the sacred circle of life. Courage is the balancing force that keeps the Rainbow together.

**Blue**—Understanding. Understanding comes when you have listened and heard the lessons in life and have applied the medicine to treat the lessons.

You have Understanding when you see the reason for the lessons in your life. Understanding comes with acceptance.

**Purple**—Knowledge. Knowledge is facts, truth, principles, awareness. It is insight, being well informed and clear. As you live your life as a two-legged, you might question a lot that goes on. Why did someone do what they did? Why did something go the way it went? Why didn't I do better when I had the chance? Knowledge is the acceptance that two-leggeds learn that fills their heart with Balance. Knowledge is your best friend, your sword and shield. Knowledge understands the facts the way they were written and what they meant to the one who wrote them. It is the ability to sit still and gather the Knowledge of where you are at and what you are up against. When you have the facts, Knowledge is present as a tool. Knowledge can only be quenched with Truth.

**Burgundy**—Will. Will is determination. It is the deliberate Power of Choice. It is desire and purpose. It is Will that sets peace in motion. It is our giving up our secrets and opening up our doors and allowing ourselves to be sure that the Will is healthy. We cannot live in wishes and dreams. We must stand in Vision, for it is purpose and that is Will. Will is our ability to make our own Choices. Will can lead to lessons and challenges. It opens doors to the Understanding of Mystery.

# AMIMAL SPIRIT TEACHINGS OF THE NORTH

**Red medicine**—Lizard. The lizard is a sign and symbol that you are facing your fear. Any time you choose to face your fear you are working with lizard medicine. It also denotes a detachment from the ego. This is a good thing for it means you are conducting yourself in a spiritual way. The lizard helps you regain the Power to deal with what you believe you have lost. The lizard gives you the ability to walk in the wintertime, controlling your dreams, and moving into the other worlds: learning from the upper world, the ancestors, and from the lower world, the teachers of your fantasies, passions, and desires.

**Red lesson**—Scorpion. The scorpion teaches you that you are embarking upon your dark and negative energies, and it shows you how to throw these dark, negative energies back on the sender. The scorpion speaks of transmutation and reveals that you have the ability to stand in your own Strength, but you must die and be reborn, making it through the hardest times in life. It shows you that the hard times in life are simply a state of mind. Scorpion lessons are the lessons of survival. They teach you that no matter what, you will survive.

**Orange medicine**—Badger. It is a good thing to look at the aggression in life as the medicine of a badger. The aggressiveness the badger walks with puts us into the Knowledge of the earth. The badger represents earth, magic and Wisdom. When you are in need, Badger medicine speaks of control. It is cunning and bold self-expression. The badger is noted as an elder because it is a storyteller, a keeper of stories, and it allows us to have creative action in a crisis. It is a symbol of the protection of rights and spiritual ideas.

**Orange lesson**—Bobcat. When you are working with the bobcat and learning the lessons of the bobcat, you will be confronted with suspicion. You will have to seek out ancient mystical mysteries and develop the ability to live in solitude. You will have the ability to see through masks, and you will walk with clear Vision in dark places. The bobcat is vigilance.

**Yellow medicine**—Dolphin. The dolphin is a keeper of Prayer, for it is the Knowledge of the sea, which is vastness. It represents Change and Wisdom, Balance, harmony, and freedom. It speaks of using the breath to release intense emotions, and Understanding the Power of rhythm in your life. The dolphin wishes us to have communication skills in prayer.

**Yellow lesson**—Seal. The seal teaches us that we cannot have our way and that we are okay when Change comes into our lives. Often when we are walking with seal lessons, we are moving through our emotions at high levels of energy. We have to accept the Wisdom of Creator in seal lessons. Through our faith, the seal tells us that we are free from danger and are not to be afraid.

**Green medicine**—Bee. The bee is the symbol of a hard worker. It opens the door to Understanding the feminine principle in life. It gives us the ability to release earthbound spirits. It is a strong medicine when dealing with prosperity. It reflects your Success and your ability to explore the actions that are mysteries in your life. It shows you that you are a true warrior. It applies the Energy of feminism to both male and female. To come into your fullest understanding, bee medicine allows you to know that you are a miracle, and that you can overcome any disarray or disconnection by having faith.

**Green lesson**—Goose. The goose teaches you to fly past your fear, not to be connected with the quagmire or be belittled by the intimidating remarks of others. The goose represents the ability to handle pride as a tool. It teaches you that there is no difference between the eagle and the goose for they are both birds. It is only what people choose to teach about the goose or the eagle that sets up a difference between them. The goose says to carry your pride and understand the Strength of your existence. The goose holds within it the Balance of the story of black and white, the beginning and the end.

**Blue medicine**—Starfish. The starfish reveals the secrets within. It says that we are to stand up and walk past our fears and live in balanced mental health. The starfish is a connection between the star people—the Colors that bring forth the teachings of Rainbow Medicine—and the watery world. These are the teachings of movement and lucidity.

**Blue lesson**—Bluebird. When times are bleak and dark and you feel as if you are on the brink of extinction, bluebird lessons bring forth the teachings of fulfillment. They allow you to feel happiness and joy in your life. The bluebird shows that you have medicine to guide your path and that nothing can destroy your soul. It is the transformation from the old to the new. It is inner joy. It is the ability to understand the transition between the physical and the spiritual.

**Purple medicine**—Trout. The trout knows its way. It picks its spot and stays very close to it. Trout shows us that we have the ability to be safe. It tells us that the spot we have chosen in life is Great Spirit, and that we are safe in the spirit world. The trout carries the colors of the rainbow. It represents the Knowledge of the Colors.

**Purple lesson**—Mule. The mule shows us that things aren't always the way we think they ought to be. We have the Choice of learning the lesson of flow or being stubborn. The mule represents stubbornness. It speaks to the fact that we don't always know our path, but if we take time to be obedient in Prayer and study, our spiritual path will be revealed to us. When on the spiritual path, we have fulfillment. We feel rich, balanced and connected.

**Burgundy medicine**—Magpie. The greatness of burgundy speaks through Understanding the Balance of light and darkness, which is the Truth of the magpie. The magpie makes friends with the wolf. They both see the darkness for what it is—a deeper shade of green, blue, purple, or burgundy. The magpie is a voice of prophecy. It speaks to us of intelligence and spirit. It wants us to listen through our Prayers to hear the good luck and fortune that Great Spirit sends our way. If you look closely at its feathers, you will see the rainbow. The white represents the purity of spirit, as the darkness represents the totality of the rainbow.

**Burgundy lesson**—Lightning bug. Lightning bugs tell us that lessons aren't always as difficult as we think they are. The light shows us the child in us is always alive. That each one of us needs fun and play. Have faith in the colors for they will flicker and glow. They will sparkle in the twilight. This is the teaching of the lightning bug. It represents spirituality.

## LESSONS OF THE NORTH

**Red**—Trust. Trust is your inner core. It is the strongest energy that human two-leggeds have for survival. To learn to trust is to stand in your greatest Strength. It is to understand that you can be relied upon and have the ability to rely on someone else. When trust has been broken, the lesson of trust is the hardest one in the wheel to learn. To trust is to know that you are safe in the light. In Trust we learn to Balance pain for sometimes in life things go the way they go. Since it all is the Will of Great Spirit, we want and need things to go the way they go. When you Trust, you accept and take from the lesson what you need and let the rest go. As you learn to Trust you see your need and hold what is dear in your memory.

**Orange**—Limits. The lesson of limits is a lesson in safety. It is much like trust. We as humankind need limits. They are our boundaries. To have a safe and good life we need to know what we can and cannot do. To set a limit is an act of self protection. When you know the boundaries and rules, you can achieve. You set the limits in your life and others set their limits. Limits are manners, respect, rules, laws, personal needs, and wants. They should be clear and well defined. Your limits keep your soul healthy.

**Yellow**—Expectations. Expectations are like quicksand. You sink into your thoughts and set habits. You expect—and that can become a set pattern of thinking. If you step into the quicksand of thoughts, your behaviors can become bad habits. If you have expectations, then they need to be expectations of Confidence, Truth, Wisdom, Choice, Real, and Courage.

Expectations can lead to the physical illness known as anxiety. The lesson of expectations is learned by applying acceptance.

**Green**—Failure. In Failure you have opportunity—the chance to start over or do it differently. It might not be like the first opportunity, but you always have another chance. No matter what it is, there is always a second time. There is always another try, a different way. We must apply Forgiveness to our life, let go of guilt and blame, and go on .The only failure is giving up.

**Blue**—Listening. To learn the lesson of listening you must be able to hear. To hear, you must be present, you must be connected, you must be mentally well, you must be open to the full examples of Strength and Confidence. When you choose to listen, remember to look at what you are listening to. Don't do more than one thing at a time when you are listening.

**Purple**—Forgiveness. Learning the lesson of forgiveness can be painful, because you cannot turn your cheek and go back into an abusive situation. Learning the lesson of forgiveness means dismissing the pain. Understanding that time has run out and that the only way you can get past painful events that call for forgiveness is to let go of the situation. Forgiveness happens when you hold no anxieties, no expectations, and choose to let go and move on. Forgiveness is not tolerating, not allowing your self to be abused, and not submitting to situations because of guilt. To forgive is to understand that people make bad choices. Ask yourself if you can accept a person's mistakes and allow them to change. If not, dismiss the person and move on, removing their presence from your life.

**Burgundy**—Inner Peace. When you have Balance in your spirit, a healthy brain, a well mind, a strong connection to spirituality, and an Understanding that your soul is your connection with Grandmother/Grandfather/Great Spirit/Creator/God, then you have inner peace. Inner peace goes beyond faith and beyond joy into the realm of the Grandmother/Grandfather/Creator/God.

# ACKNOWLEDGMENTS

My heartfelt thanks goes to C. H. Al, you are the one. Many thanks to Doc Baker, Dr. Leon, and Dr. Sybil. Dr. Eric, Sam, Dr. Catherine, Dr. Rich, and Dr. Terry, and an OLE medicine man, you are ones who made me understand and find the mental Truth. Thanks to the many great psychiatrists who have recently opened the doors to acknowledging that there is more to the human thought process than just the physical reality of the brain.

Sheila Anne Barry—You believe and listen to me when sometimes I feel it is very dark. You edit it just right and I thank you for that.

To Star Song—your voice is the song of the bluebird.

To Granny Jo—this time magic happened. The Grandmother passed to the Grandson the words of Wisdom in typed words. My Mom thanks you.

Tyler—you're standing in the doorway of being a man. Your Uncle and I see the medicine and the ways of your Nana. You are the star that made this happen, the long hours, the answers, and the long magic fingers...You are the Man!

A very special thanks to C.T. You expanded my thoughts and still do, by asking questions about the Will. I thank you for being the best friend one could have. Joe, thanks for the support!

To my loving husband, Raven. Thanks for twenty Grand years.

As I complete the circle of four directions with *Wolf Medicine*, I reflect on each and every reader and every piece of mail, and give gratitude for the Internet that allows each one of you to expand your Knowledge through the teachings that I have from within my Vision.

Aho!

**To contact the Author:**
Wolf Moondance
453 East Wonderview Avenue
P.O. Box 6000
Estes Park, CO 80517
www.wolfmoondance.com_

# INDEX

Ability, 152
Acceptance, 103, 148, 169
Addictions, 11, 162
Agreement, 126
Amulet, 76
Ancestor, 11
Anger, 136, 164, 169, 180
Animal power, 177
    Spirit teachings, 183–186
Aura, 12, 22, 163
Badger, 184
    Man, 73–83
    medicine, 83
Balance, 174
    rods of, 20
Basket of Knowledge Stones, 143–144
Beaker, 136
Bear, 30
Bear's eye, 75
Beauty, stories of, 44
Bee, 184–185
    Dancer, 106
    Medicine, 112–113
Belief, 149, 159
    systems, 167
Blaming, 9, 13, 66
Bluebird, 124–125, 130–131, 185
Blue-Eyed Raven, 30, 31, 44, 53, 81, 91, 92, 94, 95–97, 154, 158
Blue jay, 177
Blue Road, 30, 92, 158
Bobcat, 184
    baby, 80
    Woman, 74–77, 79
Bone Medicine, 7
Bottles, five, 43–46
Bowl, prayer, 177
Brain actions, 146
    and mind reality, 23
    as a mechanism, 9, 11, 12, 126
    as knowing, 146

    damage to, 164
Breath, 9
Buffalo medicine, 76
    totem of the North, 50
    Woman, White, 44
Buffalo's eye, 75
Bumblebee, 110
Candles, 22
Centerology, 93
Ceremony, 64, 71
    of Clearing the Mind, 179–180
    of Courage, 114–115
    of Soul Recovery, 163–164
    of the Inner Wolf, 139–142
    of the Medicine Bundle, 70–71
    of the Sacred Herbs, 22
    of the Soul, 127–130
    of the Spirit Warrior, 64–67
Chakra heart and solar plexus, 22
    system, 163
    third eye, 22;
    throat, 36
Chakras, 149, 174
Chart of Color, Animal, Medicine, and
    Lesson Words, 86
Chemical
    imbalances, 11, 139, 149, 164, 168
    reaction, 76
Chicken, 177
Choice, 152, 153, 159
Christianity, 13
Clearing the Mind, Ceremony of, 179–180
Cold, head, 38
Color, 181
    Medicine Bundle, 55, 67–71
    teachings, 62–63
Colors, meanings of the, 181–183
Computer, 22
Confidence, 36
Confusion, 29
Courage, 106, 108, 110, 182

Ceremony of, 114–115
  teachings of, 112–113
Coyote, 29, 30
Creativity, 32
Creator, face of the, 153
Crow, 177
  story of the, 25–26
Crystal, 20–21
  rods, 19–21
Dark Eyes, 26–31, 46, 53, 78, 79, 83, 91, 92, 95, 107–108, 110, 134, 158, 171
Dark Heart, 77–83, 91
Dark night, 134, 149
Darkness, 135
Death, 9, 12, 20–21, 41, 58
Deliberate action, 152
Denial, 118, 139
Depression, 11, 112–113 139
Desire, 152, 153
Determination, 152
Directions, 50, 76, 86
  color, 88
Dolphin, 93, 94, 184
  medicine, 98
Donkey Man, 136
Dreaming Lizard, 55
Eagle, 177
  Woman, White, 44
Eagle's eye, 75
Eight, in the spirit world, 48
Eldership, 9, 21
Emotions, 9, 12, 112
  runaway, 110
Energy, 74, 182
  balance of, 87
  leak, 89, 111
  teachings of, 83
Evil, 12
Expectations, 92–94
  exercise in the lesson of, 103
  lesson of, 102–103, 186–187
Failure, lesson of, 110, 115–118, 187
Fear, 13, 112–113, 115, 125, 126, 135, 169, 176
Feather, 177
Feelings, 9
Fire — the caretaker, 34
Fireflies, 47
Footprint, animal, 87

Forgiveness
  lesson of, 133, 148, 187
  voice of the soul, 158
Four Crows, Grandmother, 93
Fun, 153
Goose, 177, 185
Medicine, 115–118
Granny Smith, 175
Gray Wolf, 91–96
Great Spirit connection to, 145
  will of, 155–156, 158
Ground — the worker, 34
Grudges, 164
Guide, inner spirit, 35
Habits, 139, 148
Happiness, spirit of, 174
Harmonics, 174, 176
Hate, 12
Hawk, 177
Headcold, 38
Healing, 32, 64, 98
Heart, 10, 12, 126
  chakra, 38
  talk, 95
Hollow bone, 17, 50
Hoofprint, 87
Horse's eye, 75
Humility, 131
Ignorance, 13
Illness, 10–11, 125
Inner peace, lesson of, 168–169, 187
Inner spirit guide, 35
Inner Wolf, Ceremony of, 139–142
Interpretation, 124–125
Journal, 22, 32
King Coyote, 79, 92, 110, 112, 113, 158
Knowing, 147, 153
  spiritual, 144
Knowledge, 183
  teachings of, 139
Lessons, 32, 50
  of the North, 10
Lifekind, 8
Light beings, 153
Lightning bug, 156, 157, 168–169
Limits, lesson of, 80, 84, 186
Listening, lesson of, 124–125, 130–131, 187
Lizard, 183

bundle, 156
  medicine, 62–63
Lower world, 161
Lynx's eye, 75
Magpie, 154, 158–159; 177, 185–186
Mare Woman, White, 44
Marriage pot, 93, 94, 97, 99–102
Meanness, 59
Medicine as a word, 22
  blanket, 22
  Bundle, Color, 67–71
  wheel, 10, 49–50
  teachings of the, 47
Medicines, 50
  of the North, 10
Memory, 139, 142
Mental illness, 10, 13, 164
Middle world, 161
Mind, open, 159
  understandings guided by the, 147
Mind: 9–10
  actions of the, 146;
  and brain, 7–11
  as home of spirit and soul, 12
Moons, twenty-eight, 122
Mouse, assistant to the wolf, 50
Mule, the, 148, 185
Neck cloth, 35–39
Neurology, 149
Numbers, frequencies of, 174
Old Stick Woman, 54–62
Opportunity, 116–117, 153
Owl Woman, White, 44
Owl, 177
Passion and romance, 29, 79, 81, 89, 103, 108, 127, 171
Path, sacred, 32–35
Perpetual motion, 9
Physicality, 7
Pineal gland, 7
Pleiades, the, 44
Post-traumatic stress, 112
Prayer, 32, 44, 64, 182
  bowl, 177–179
  daily, 149
  teachings of, 98, ties 98–99
Purpose, 152, 153
Queen of Hearts, 92
Rainbow, 134

Bridge, 11, 31, 53
Medicine Wheel, 8–9, 47–51, 171
Path, 156, 177
Raven, 177
  song of the, 44, 47
  Woman, White, 44
  see Blue-Eyed Raven
Raven's eye, 75
Red Road, 30, 92
  good, 33, 139, 156, 177, 178
River People, 135
Robe, dropping your, 41
Romance. See Passion and romance
Sacred Clans, 75
Sacred
  path, 32–35
  Sight, 75
  spiral, 174
Sage, 22, 23
Scorpion, 59–61, 183–184
  medicine, 63–64
Seal, 94, 184
  medicine, 102–103
Seals, lesson of the, 93
Self esteem, low, 162
Seven Seers, 75
Shaman, 8
Shamanic journey as soul retrieval exercise, 163–165
  vision, 7
Shamanism, 13, 23
Sickness, 10–11, 180
Silver cord, 127
Sky — the dreamer, 34
Smells of existence, 43, 47
Smith, Granny, 175
Smudging, 22
Snabbers, 59–62, 106, 109–111
Soul mates, 91–93, 95, 110
Soul, 11, 12, 126, 139
  and spirit, 161
  Ceremony of the, 127–130
  dark night of, 134
  destruction of a, 162
  healthy, 145, 162
  knowing, 139
  path of Truth and Confidence, 134
  pathway of the spirit, 144–145, 160, 161
  Recovery, Ceremony of, 163–164

Retrieval, 107, 159–168
   exercise, 165–168
   journey, 164–165
   seven movements of the, 160–161
Spirit, 12, 62, 126, 144
   and soul, 161
   Ceremony of, 64–67
   feet, 160
   guide, 35
   Keepers, 75–76, 86
   lights, 157
   one of all, 34
   rejected, 149
   voice of, 159
   walk, 35
   Warrior, 56–58
Spiritual knowing, 144
Starfish, 120–121, 185
   as totem for Understanding Medicine, 124–126
   one, 121–122
Stars — the storyteller, 34
Stones
   as tools in shamanic work, 23
   knowledge, 143–144
Sun dance, 171
Sweet grass, 22, 23
Sweet Medicine, 30, 49, 77, 151, 157, 170–178
Tah-no-he, 73–83
Tape recorder, 22
Teaching stick, 70
Third eye, 75
Thoughts, 93
Time, 46
Tools, spiritual, 22–23
Totem

animals, 86, 87
spiral, 86–87
Transformation, 20
Trinity, 50
Trout, 133, 185
   Medicine, 139
Trust, lesson of, 63–64, 186
Truth, lack of facing, 153
Turkey, 177
Turq, 19–21
Turtle Island, 171
Twigs, Grandmother, 54–62
Understanding, 124, 182
   teachings of, 125–126
Upper world, 161
Vision, 131
Voice, as teacher, 17, 20
Walk, spirit, 35
Wa-Na-Shoshie, 75–77
Water — one of flow, 34
Waterfall, 153–154
Will, 183
   teachings of, 158–159
Wind — the ancient one, 34
Witchcraft, 13
Wolf
   as teacher, 17
   Ceremony of the Inner, 139–142
   compared to Coyote, 29
   job of the, 7
   role of the, 9
   teachings, 181–187
   totem of the North, 50
   Woman, White, 44
Wolf's Eye, 75; amulet, 85–89
Wrinkle-face, 172
Zanday, 174